Living Reality
The Loving Presence of God

Marie M. Constance

Copyright © 2014 Marie M. Constance
All rights reserved.

ISBN: 0615989608
ISBN-13: 9780615989600
Library of Congress Control Number: 2014905376
Margaret Sigrist, Pocomoke City, MD

To my mother.

Along the Shores of Forever

How nice was my solitary walk by the sea—
Solitary, perhaps to the eye
Of a passerby,
But only to that sense
So often misconstrued
As a bearer of truth.

Another sense more sublime
Would tell another tale,
One that ironically
Must here be told
And thus heard
Through the same sense
That in the eye is transferred.

My pen will tell
Your heart this tale
As you read these written words,
But my purpose is to reveal
The truth not told
By passersby
Who saw one walking alone,
But by my Lord God's step beside me
To be yet felt and known.

He talked to me
Of continuous,
Uninterrupted
Oneness
As we walked
Hand in hand,
Heart in heart

Along the shore.
He talked to me
Of love,
Of loving,
Of being loved
As we walked
Arm in arm,
Head to head
Along the shore.

He talked to me
Of beauty
And light
And glory
As we walked
Eye to eye,
Ear to ear
Along the shore.

He talked to me
Of tenderness
And sweetness
And joy
As we walked
Beloved and beloved,
Soul and soul,
Spirit in spirit,
Body in body
My God and me,
He and I,
One in one
Always, always, always
Together
Along the shores of forever.

Acknowledgments

I wish to express my heartfelt gratitude to those who have loved, supported, and encouraged me in the process of writing this book, especially my husband, our children, my family, and dear friends. Through each and all I have realized the profound truth that God comes to us in the guise of our loved ones. I am also indebted to my dear benefactor and the editors, designers, and other staff at CreateSpace. I am sincerely grateful to all who make this volume accessible to those who may read it and receive the message of love it holds.

Contents

Background   xv
I will make your dreams a living reality.

Introduction   xxix
*I am guiding your pen. I am holding your heart.
I am loving you, My dear.*

Lesson One: Think Me   1
*Think Me while you are performing any action.
Try to think of Me.*
    Chapter One   3
    Chapter Two   8

Lesson Two: Acceptance with Humility
Goes Hand in Hand with Trust   29
*Let peace settle upon your heart, My dear,
as you accept humbly and trust.*
    Chapter Three   31
    Chapter Four   36
    Chapter Five   53

Lesson Three: Remain   69
Remain, My child, in Me. Remain steadfast in Me.
    Chapter Six   71
    Chapter Seven   75
    Chapter Eight   86

Lesson Four: Receive and Be Open   103
Receive and be open, My dear,
so My love will flow through,
My words will be heard,
and My word will be known.
     Chapter Nine   105
     Chapter Ten   109
     Chapter Eleven   125

Lesson Five: Manifest   141
I wish for you to make known My love.
I wish for you to make known My joy.
     Chapter Twelve   143
     Chapter Thirteen   148
     Chapter Fourteen   166

Lesson Six: Remain in My Loving You   185
Let Me reveal Myself to you in this, My loving you.
     Chapter Fifteen   187
     Chapter Sixteen   190
     Chapter Seventeen   209

Lesson Seven: Balance   229
I will come to you in your work, My child,
and I will come to you in your meditation,
but you must learn to balance your life.
     Chapter Eighteen   231
     Chapter Nineteen   236
     Chapter Twenty   261

Lesson Eight: Stay   277
Stay in My joy. Stay in My love.
Stay in My embrace.
     Chapter Twenty-one   279

Chapter Twenty-two 284
Chapter Twenty-three 298

A Divine Plea 309
Let Me care for you. Let Me love you.

Background
I will make your dreams a living reality.

I was born into a very loving family. My earliest memories are of happily playing with my brothers, neighborhood kids, and pets. I don't recall ever being worried about anything other than mosquito bites and a few knee scrapes that wouldn't heal because I kept falling on the sidewalk, reopening them over and over. My parents provided me with many playmates, both boys and girls. I learned how to care for young children by watching and helping my mother, who amazes me more now that I am a mother than while I was growing up. How did she do it? Anyway, I had a happy, healthy, carefree childhood, never really concerned about anything outside of my family or school except for one thing: God.

I remember thinking about what people said about God, that He had no beginning and no end, and that He had created the world and all the people and plants and animals, and the sun and moon and stars too. That He had a son whose name was Jesus, and there was also a Holy Ghost that sometimes looked like a white bird, kind of like a sea gull, but they said it was a dove. I didn't know what a dove looked like, but I accepted it all quite as a matter of fact because they said so.

Then there was Christmas, that time of year when my brothers and I went crazy from all the excitement—not so much because of that story about God's baby being born but because we got presents, the kind we didn't get at any other time of year. Excitement was everywhere; for us it was about Santa Claus and his reindeer coming to our house. We actually saw evidence of sleigh tracks in the snow one Christmas morning. I now wonder how my parents managed to handle it all, for the thrill was almost more than we could bear.

As I grew a little older, I listened more to the other Christmas story, the one about God's baby. I felt sorry for the mother and father having to spend the night in a stable, and that part about there being no room at the inn struck me as odd because it was God's baby, not just any baby, being born. I wondered what it must have been like for those shepherds when they saw all that light and all those angels, how those kings came so far to find the baby, and how bright that star must have been. I wondered a great deal about that story in the midst of all the fun and excitement of Christmas.

I used to wonder about other stories concerning God too, especially His having no beginning and no end, which I just could not understand. I tried to think back in time, or forward as far as I was able, but I still could not grasp such a concept. My grandfather told me I used to ask him profound questions about God at a very early age. I don't remember that. I just remember playing hard every day and occasionally wondering about the world…and God.

My parents taught us to say our prayers every night before going to bed. I'm not sure when it started, but I used to think it made God happier if I kneeled instead of staying in bed while saying my prayers. So many nights I'd be comfortably in my covers, drifting off to sleep, when suddenly I'd realize I forgot to say my prayers. Then I'd go through the thing about kneeling, being tempted at first to stay in my covers but knowing all along I would have to get out of bed to pray. If I didn't, I'd be sorry because I wanted to make God happier.

Now, don't misunderstand: it wasn't because I feared God or thought He would punish me or even be disappointed. No, none of those things entered my thinking about the God of whom I had heard and formed my own concept. I just wanted to make Him happier. I wanted to please Him in my own little way. I'm not sure if this kind of thinking came

Living Reality

from my parents' guidance, from something I had heard from someone else, or from my heart and soul. All I can tell is that as far back as I can remember, my concept of God was one of love. I felt certain of God's love for me, and I simply wanted to return the same.

As time went on, I started thinking more about Jesus—not so much of the baby anymore but of the man. I remember concluding that Jesus had made Himself really tiny to fit inside us, and he was pushing all the buttons to make our bodies work. That really seemed to make sense out of what "they" said. I guess I just couldn't grasp the concept of His fitting inside, helping and guiding us, any other way. As I grew older, though the notion of Jesus's being in me in spirit didn't make any more sense, I had to toss out the earlier, childish explanation I had formed on my own. I became a bit aggravated by all the things they said about God and Jesus. It just didn't make sense. So often I used to wish I had lived when Jesus was on Earth. Then I could have gotten some answers!

I used to think about things like having a genie or a magic ring or anything that would grant me wishes. I'd think of so many things it would be fun to have, or for which I could wish for my family, others, or even the poor people I kept hearing about, who seemed to need everything. Then I'd play the game where I would have only one wish. What would I say? I'm not sure when it started, but afterward I never changed what had become my favorite wish: that I could talk to Jesus and Jesus would talk to me. Then I could understand everything. I could ask Him all the questions I had. I could ask Him anything, and He wouldn't mind or think me foolish because He loved me.

I started imagining what that would be like. I began wanting to meet Him more than to talk to Him, to be with Him and to be friends. How comforting that would have been. I can still feel how I felt when I used to imagine being with Him—it was so sweet, so refreshing, and so enjoyable. As I think about my childhood wish now, what comes to mind is probably the same image that came so often all those years ago. I dreamed of myself as a young girl, walking and talking hand in hand with Jesus through meadows, along streams, through the woods, on a day as beautiful as the first mild day of spring. There were blue skies, white fluffy clouds, warm sunshine, and birds singing, and He was looking down at me and smiling. That's what I used to wish for more than anything in the whole world, and, as incredible as it may seem, now my wish has come true!

As an adolescent I was involved in the usual things: family, friendships, school, sports, church, and jobs. Through it all, I remember, I was very frustrated by the way people couldn't seem to get along because of their differences. It used to bother me, and I even got up in front of the entire class in the auditorium and tried to explain how it would be so much better if we didn't form groups or cliques. I felt quite embarrassed and foolish the more I tried to put into words what I thought the problem was with people and why we weren't getting along. As I think back, I remember the other students' faces; they looked as if they were thinking, "What is she talking about?" I also remember a very sympathetic look from one of the faculty, as if she were saying both to me and to herself, "It is a shame, isn't it? But don't be too discouraged."

Anyway, my adolescent years were fun and exciting, but underlying it all was that longing to dissolve the differences that seemed to cause so much strife among so many. Another longing that haunted my inner life was to find some answers that really made sense, answers to those age-old questions such as: Who is God? Where is God when people are having so much trouble living? Why can't people get along? What should I do about all this? When will I understand God better? And what is love?

Then I fell in love. How wonderful! All those questions, except the last, lost their hold on my heart for a while. My only concern was that wonderful new feeling and the person for and with whom I felt it. As time went on, the questions began to surface again, but I had someone with whom I could talk about them. Life had a new dimension: all I thought, all I felt, all I learned, all I feared, and all for which I longed included my newfound love. We sought answers together. Being in love was such an awakening for me! I discovered poetry and enjoyed exploring numerous poets' musings on the wonders of love. What pleasure and satisfaction I found in their spellbinding verses and knowing their meanings.

Living Reality

In a few years we were married. We soon found that life held yet another dimension for us: our first child was born. There are no words to describe such a tremendous blessing. I can only say if you have children, you must understand; if you do not, I wish you could. I wish all could know such wonder, such joy, and such a miracle. After our daughter was born, my husband and I looked at each other but were speechless. We could only feel and share the deepest affirmation of our beings and our love through mutual smiles and tears. Such tears of joy. Oh, thank You, God!

We searched even more for meaning, to express our individual as well as our shared gratitude, and to know more of this God who had gifted us so. We read, we prayed, we searched, and we discussed. We were regular participants in the Catholic Mass, yet we yearned for more. The books we found to be most appealing were those dealing with the universality of God, with the underlying truths of all religions: that God is one, and God is love. We hungered for more books that would reveal the experience of God within as the basic connecting thread in all religions. That knowledge of God, which is firsthand—that is, experienced within one's heart and soul—is what we wanted to find for ourselves.

We found a way through the writings of a man of God from India. He came to America in order to teach any sincere seeker of God, no matter of what background or religion, how to find inner communion with God. In a spirit of humility and reverence for God in all faiths, this man offered his wisdom to all. We read one of his books and felt drawn to his profound love of God and his wisdom as well as his sincere love for humankind. Because his writings were so inspiring, we wrote to the organization he had founded to learn more. As we learned basic meditation techniques, we began to make the search for God within us a daily part of our life together.

As the years went on, we tried to balance the demands of everyday life with the desire to find God and to live in His presence. Our family grew; we were gifted with three more children. As we adjusted our daily routines often, our spiritual search evolved as well. We persisted in the practice of meditation and continued to participate in the Catholic faith, raising our children in our own blend of East and West. Being very much aware of the tendency among people to be closed to and even critical of such a diversion from tradition, we kept our beliefs within the privacy of our home, sharing only with those with whom we felt affinities and the same approach to God.

Though my love of and for my husband and our children had brought new meaning to my life, I continued to search for deeper meaning in my relationship with God. My yearning for God underscored my practice of meditation, prayer life, and daily activities. I longed for that loving relationship about which I had read and heard, and I prayed with all my heart and soul for God to let me know Him.

I wrote about my feelings for God in letters to a close friend, confiding my heart's deepest yearnings. Often I would break into song and write prayers and poems about my love for God and my longing to know Him. As I experienced God's response, my writing increased in both volume and intensity, yet because those writings were so sacred and precious to my being, I shared them with only a few close friends.

I began to have glimpses of that for which I had been yearning: the sweet presence of God within me. My yearnings took on new dimensions, and as I found my heart aflame with such love for this indwelling Lord, I begged Him to show me how to love Him more. One day, which I recall as quite ordinary (though it was far from ordinary!), He broke His long silence. I remember it as if it were yesterday. I had desired His presence, which I had been discovering more steadily in the silence and stillness of meditation, yet being the mother of small children, I could not just stop everything to go practice.

I heard a voice speaking to me: *Don't you know I am always with you? You need not go anywhere or sit at your altar. I am ever in your heart and soul, but you must realize the work you are doing for your children and your dear husband is for Me. You are working for Me in all you do no matter how small the task.*

For about twelve years, I heard the same voice speaking to me, on the average every six months or so. Everything I heard I recorded in my journals, but I did not know what to believe. I doubted that God was actually talking to me and even thought I had imagined it all, or that I was crazy. Because of the doubts, I did not tell anyone about hearing the voice until one day when it all changed, and I heard the following words: *You see, My child, I want your every happiness. It is only in your letting go and opening up to My way—in your not limiting Me—that I may thus give to you more fully. By your not limiting Me, you open yourself up to unlimited possibilities. You are waiting not for what you want to write but for that which I want you to write. Struggle not with your own writing. Let Me dictate to you. Then and only then will you write what is right.*

It all changed because of my response, although that wasn't immediate. Actually, in an attitude of combined fear and disbelief, I wrote those very words above on a small piece of paper and put them in the back of my desk, only to discover them again two months later. Then I shared those words with a very close friend, who encouraged me to believe the voice I had heard was the voice of God.

Such belief marked a turning point in my life as I decided all I had heard and would hear from this voice, I would receive and record as God's messages to me. Feeling a stirring deep within, I began to look at those writings differently. Searching through twelve years of writings, I marked all that were of this nature—that is, from another, or conversations between that other and me—and compiled them all in one place. How I was in awe! They took on new meaning and made me cry even to think these words could be God's...God's! I was deeply touched, deeply moved, deeply affected, and, I think, deeply changed by that one possibility that became more and more convincing the more I wrote.

Several months later I felt as if God had something in store for me or something to tell me. Feeling pulled to go for a walk along a mountain stream, I did so and found a nice haven where I sat, prayed, and listened. Oh, to drink in the sweetness of the sound of a running brook! When I asked, "Can You tell me now, Lord, what it is?"

He replied, *I want you to publish a book* and requested I prayerfully reread all my writings and select prayer reflections and conversations to include in such a book. My heart danced, and I melted in a wave of sweetness and gratitude that flowed into a wave of joy and anticipation of more wonders to come.

Though the conversations were at first short and typically limited to the matter of my coming to believe in them as real, as they became more frequent and lengthy, their themes grew more diverse and expansive. In the beginning the conversations occurred whenever I would choose to write. As time went on, whenever I heard Him initiating a conversation, I would respond in thought first and then write that down and continue to write any words in our ensuing conversation. In that way I developed the habit of writing often.

Desiring that the conversations with Him increase, I initiated more often. The conversations He initiated also became more frequent. At first He addressed me as *My child* and then *My dear* until one wonderful day, I heard Him say my name. How I melted! He often began by making a request or by telling me something in answer to my thoughts, which were not initially directed at Him. I began to converse with Him without the use of my pen, but I longed to write everything down. Often I stopped whatever I was doing so I could record the conversations. This was frustrating at times as I had to fulfill my daily obligations, yet I felt as well the longing to please Him by writing His words. He assured me He would continue to converse with me whether or not I recorded it, and if He desired the words to be written He would guide me toward writing. He promised to help me with balancing my daily life, often reassuring me if I felt frustrated. I came to realize that in writing or performing any activity, as long as I did it for Him, I was pleasing Him. My frustration subsided and was replaced by a sweet contentment. Written or not, the conversations became part of my daily life.

Now, whenever I think of my Lord, I know He is listening to my thoughts, and whenever I speak to Him within in my mind, I feel His presence. Actually I feel He is always here within me. His companionship is constant, and though we are not always conversing in words, most all of my thinking includes Him or always returns to Him. If I am in a place that requires little or no concentration, I find myself automatically turning toward Him like a compass turning its needle north. When I have a question, I ask Him directly, and He usually answers with words, although often the answer is not what I expected. I frequently tell

Him how beautiful the world is and thank Him for such beauty as well as for all I hold dear, and for many little things all throughout the day that I believe happen by His hand's touch.

As for the conversations, they occur all day and even in the night should I awaken. I talk to Him; I listen to Him. I talk with Him; I listen with Him. My voice is my thinking directed to Him within me, although if I'm alone I sometimes use my audible voice. His voice is another thinking kind of voice, but it is not mine. I have come to recognize the person behind that voice, and I feel His presence first and always before I hear it. His voice is clear and gentle, kind and tender, cheerful and wise, often witty or funny, and playful too. These are all attributes of His personality that come through when He speaks and in His choice of words.

Isn't this incredible? I'm writing about talking with God! And I'm writing about it as if it were the most normal thing in the world, an ordinary part of every day. Perhaps that is the reason for my telling you this, to reveal how profoundly simple, normal, and ordinary it all is. Maybe that's how it's supposed to be. Maybe this is the desired norm that God wishes to be real for all His children.

I once questioned Him about this very matter: "My Lord, it is with both awe and gratitude that I record in this book this most blessed communication with You, my Lord and my life forever! It is at times inconceivable that this is truly happening. Yet why not? Why should there not be free communication between a creator and the created? It is the most natural of realities, is it not?"

He replied, *Yes, it is. Open communication is but one aspect of the truest of all realities, the one reality: I am one. You are in Me...all are in Me...thus all are in one...and most wonderful is this truth that all are one...all is one...one is all...one is. I am. I am! Come, My child. Come. Know this one reality. Then you will know all realities that are contained in the one. Come. I await your knowing. In this knowing shall arise all your loving. Thus you shall be that which I long for you to become knowingly. Come...realize...know...be!*

I exclaimed, "Oh my Jesus, my divine beloved. Lead me in. Awaken me!"

Then He responded, *Awaken thyself, My precious little one. Awaken thyself. Come!* Later He assured me, *I will make your dreams a living reality.*

In another conversation I told Him, "Lord, sometimes I am surprised by Your choice of words."

I was consoled by His explanation: *Why should I speak any differently to you than you would speak to Me? What better way for you to understand than in your own language? I use your thoughts and your language to reveal My words to you. To reveal My meaning to you I also use your heart. Keep your heart ever pure and ever aware of Me. I love you, My child!*

He has often instructed me to *come in* first *then write*. Once He said, *I have much for you to write, My dear.*

I asked, "What do You want me to write about today, my Lord?"

He replied, *You will know, My dear. You will know. First, you must come in. Come in, and let Me fill you with Myself. Be assured the essence will come through the writings.* Another time He said, *Remember: I am the one guiding your pen. Always come in before you write, and breathe My name as you write.*

When He asks me to *come in*, I stop whatever I am doing, or if that is not possible I simply change my attention to focusing on Him and the feeling of His presence within me. I try to find a place that is quiet and comfortable if possible. If it's not then I must try to focus amid distraction. If standing, I try to stand erect, or if sitting, the same, but with hands either folded in my lap or upturned in a gesture of openness. Then, with eyes closed, I call on Him by saying His name and then breathe deeply, synchronizing my breathing with repeating His name: "Je" with the in breath and "sus" with the out breath. He has referred to this as *breathing My name* and has often asked me to breathe His name deeply three times as a method of calming myself and putting myself in His presence.

His person is very clear whenever He asks me to *come in*. I do not mean visually clear, but in my being I am able to recognize that He is present. I just know it is my God. There is a certain quality to this

Living Reality

knowing. As I center myself, I focus on this knowing and on Him. I listen...I breathe...I rest...in Him. Usually I feel an increase in the flow of sweetness and energy. My love for Him intensifies, and I long just to love. Sometimes certain dear ones come into the knowing too. I feel their presence in my heart, and thoughts of them enter my mind. Other times there is an all-inclusive awareness of all people. I feel love for anyone who enters my mind and heart, and that love increases as He breathes His life and love into me. As He breathes His very self into me (*let Me fill you with Myself*), I become full—oh, so full! I want to remain in this fullness for the rest of my life.

How nice that I know He wants this too because once He said, *How nice that we want the same thing.* When I feel so full of this love, I feel happy at the same time. It is a happiness that is not dependent on anything external, rather it comes from within. I become so content in the love of God that I wonder why I ever worry about anything. I am so aware of who He is: God! Creator and sustainer of the universe. Lover of all that is. I realize I am in touch with God, and He embraces and loves me. What a wondrous living reality!

Sometimes in this coming in, I am aware of another kind of being wherein I am still or I am so absorbed in this love and this loving that I feel as if at any moment I may fly away. That hasn't happened, but I wouldn't be surprised if it did, so great and so intense is this experience of happiness supreme, this love divine, this wondrous joy of being.

Once, after prompting me with *Breathe My name deeply three times*, He asked, *What comes in this for you?*

I replied, "I feel increased devotion to You, sweeter love for You, and clearer perceptions of You."

He instructed me further: *Yes, My dear, remember this. If you have only a little time, simply breathe My Name deeply at least three times. Then relax in what wells up within you. Be in this and receive in this. This is how you may begin even now to go deeper and remain in My loving you. I am loving you all the time. You become more aware of this as you relax in My name's blessing. You always feel an increase in love when you breathe My name, don't you? Tell Me, My dear, what else you feel increasing.*

I replied, "I feel a lightness of being spreading, filling, permeating. I feel sweetness increasing all throughout my being, and I feel warmth increasing in my heart first, and then it too spreads and fills. I feel peace increasing, Lord, and happiness. Joy bubbles up from within me and seems to overflow. You already mentioned love—oh, love! How it consumes me. How I then desire to give of this love, to remain in this love, to love this love that I know is You. Thus I desire to love You, my Jesus, You who are love itself!"

His explanation and invitation followed: *My dear, this is flying. You shall fly higher yet, My dear, for this is only the beginning. Come, dear, now fly again, this time without your pen.*

I could reply only, "Yes, Lord, yes!"

After at least three deep breaths, I continued to breathe His Name with normal breaths, and when I kept my eyes closed my breathing became calmer and slower. I have found that simply taking a few moments in the midst of activity to *come in* brings calmness and quiets the mind. In that calming I become aware of God's presence within me. Because this practice has become part of the writing process, I trust in the authenticity of what comes through my pen after *coming in*.

Once He asked me, Are you any more assured of My words today?

I replied, "Yes, Lord, I am."

He inquired, *Yet have I spoken of this anymore? From where does the reassurance come? If not from My words then what?*

I answered, "From within, my Lord, from within my depths where I find You and where I find Your solace, Your presence, Your love."

He reminded me, *There. Do you see why I ask you to come? Always, always come within for the truth. If you are not sure of the words, be sure of what comes in the silence. You will know the truth in Me. When I am in you, you will know the truth. I know your thoughts. Just trust Me, My dear. Leave all to Me.*

I pleaded with Him, saying, "Yes, Lord. Just guide me and let me hear only Your voice and Your ways."

He assured me with, *So be it. I am ever your guide. If doubt or uncertainty should cause you strife, then simply call My name. Sweetly, sweetly call My name, and then calmly, calmly breathe My name. All shall melt into the peace of My presence. I shall hold you and whisper your name as you breathe Mine. Love Me, My dear, in all you meet, in all your dears, in your very heart and soul. Love Me.*

This practice of *coming in* is invaluable to prayer and writing and to any activity, creative or otherwise, including reflective reading. So perhaps it would be beneficial for you, the reader of this book, to engage in a similar practice—one that would involve some type of relaxation and centering—prior to reading the prayers and conversations that follow. You may discover, much to your delight, that a meditative preparation may actually increase your receptivity while reading and, in turn, open doors to a deeper understanding of the meaning in the words. Allow me to quote the source: *Empty...empty...empty...then enter and receive!*

In my concept of God, the Father, the Son, and the Spirit are one. I believe the one God reveals Himself to us in ways we can understand, or personalizes Himself so we may relate to Him. Although I choose to use the masculine pronouns He, Him, and His, I believe that God may be whatever is most pleasing to each one of us in our particular relationship with Him. God may be the father, the mother, the lover, the brother, the sister, the friend, the child, or the spirit without any limitation of gender, role, or form. This is my understanding, and I am not trying to debate the knowledge of theologians or of anyone who may know more about this than I do. I am merely trying to give a background of my concepts and spirituality so as to better relate my growth and experiences to you.

I simply want to share this wonderful, living reality with you because of the love that is inside me, pushing all the buttons and making me work. I call this love by name: Jesus. You may identify with the same love, the essence of this love, using the same or another name, such as Yahweh, Allah, Krishna, or Buddha, or you may give no limit of person by any name. Do not religions the world over profess and proclaim God is love?

I offer my story and all these writings to anyone who longs to know this God of love. Having received an incredible gift, I am compelled to share its wealth with my fellow human beings. Regardless of background, gender, race, culture, religion, or standing in this life, all people on Earth are my brothers and sisters. I sincerely believe that God is essentially the same all over the world. A different face, cloak, temple, or creed does not change the essence of God, the creator and lover of all humankind!

The purpose of this book is to show that God loves all and longs for all to receive Him in the very essence, the living reality of ever-present, ever-constant Love Divine. It is with the highest joy that I turn the pages of this book over to you, who may be, as I have been, searching for deeper meaning in life. Having found such meaning in this essence, and in testimony to all I have heard and received, I proclaim: Divine Love is within and is offered to all if only all would receive it. Once again I quote the source: *Receive! Receive!*

Introduction

I am guiding your pen. I am holding your heart.
I am loving you, My dear.

Over the course of a few years, I received eight lessons from God. Each stands on its own and leads into the next, but each is connected to all the other lessons as well. Lesson one, think Me, might otherwise be called "keep your mind on God." Lesson two, acceptance with humility goes hand in hand with trust, implies that an attitude of humble acceptance is essential to trusting in God. To remain, as in lesson three, is to live in awareness of God's constant loving presence.

The message in lesson four is to maintain an attitude of unhindered receptivity in order to receive and be open to God's love. Lesson five, manifest, is a turning point where the ethereal essence that comes from being open begins to take form through acts of love. In lesson six, remain in My loving you, although the focus seems to be turning to outward manifestation, there is an increased awareness of God's love within yet in a more active way. Notice the word *loving* is a verb, or an action word, as opposed to *love*, a noun, or a being word.

Lesson seven, balance, teaches the wisdom in meeting the demands of daily living while striving toward spiritual growth. Finally, even though lesson eight, stay, may be the culmination of the understanding achieved through practice of the first seven lessons, it is also a point at which there is a continuum. In other words rather than a linear teaching, these lessons are circular and flow in and out of each other in meaning as well as significance.

Although He introduced the lessons to me in sequential order, they are not necessarily sequential in the applications of their meanings in my life. He first addressed the nature of the relationship between each lesson and the others in lesson three when He said, *These lessons shall continue, My dear, and each shall flow into the next, but each shall also continue, becoming a part of the next.* Later He explained, *You are constantly learning all the lessons I give you.* For example, even though I may be focusing on balancing my daily activities with prayer and meditation, I am at the same time trying to keep my thoughts attuned to Him, thus working on lessons seven and one at once.

Although there are many other examples of how the lessons are intertwined in my daily efforts to follow His teachings, I will not cite specific examples here. I would, however, like to point out that in trying to understand each lesson as He first gave it to me, I focused primarily on that particular lesson, yet as I became more familiar with each I was able then to focus on more than one lesson at a time. Now I see how the lessons are not independent of each other, rather they are interrelated and intersect one another constantly, almost like an intertwining of several helices at once, where the constant is He!

This book is divided into eight sections with writings corresponding in theme to each of the eight lessons. The first chapter of each lesson serves as an introduction with reflections on that particular lesson. The chapters that follow within each lesson include conversations with God, each of which is preceded by a prayer in poetic form. After I recorded the following conversation, He asked me to use it in the introduction to this book *for the benefit of others.* I offer it now to you.

☙ ❧

My dear child, what do you think of all this? Tell Me. I want you to tell Me.
  "Lord, You know my thoughts, but since You've asked, I will tell You. I am truly amazed that this is happening. I am so filled with gratitude

for this revelation of Your love. I honestly think all this is absolutely wonderful! I think *You* are absolutely wonderful. I think You are the most gracious, most kind, most understanding, most gentle, most forgiving, most compassionate, most wise, most truthful, most loving, most joyful, most wonderful person. Yes, person! One who is the most anyone could ever dream of and more. You, my wonderful Lord, are all this, and, beyond my wildest dreams, You are all this to me. That is what I think."

That is why I asked. I wanted you to write it for the benefit of others, and this, My dear, shall be the introduction to your book. Now I am all this to you, but you have grown into this. You have awakened into this reality. You shall begin with now, and then, through your writings, you shall record the process of this awakening, this growth. Fear not—I will guide you. You will know what I want of you. For now I want you to know I am guiding your pen. I am holding your heart. I am loving you, My dear.

☙ ❧

All that follows in this book flows from the process mentioned above—my awakening into that blessed living reality. I invite you to enter and receive the same.

Lesson One: Think Me

*Think Me while you are performing any action.
Try to think of Me.*

Chapter One

Oh, to keep the mind on God at all times! What a challenge it is to strive for such a goal while countless distractions and stimuli are ever influencing my thoughts. When I first heard His words—*Today we shall begin lesson one: think Me*—I wondered why He did not simply say *think of Me* or *think about Me*. As the meaning of the first lesson unfolded, I realized He did ask me to think of Him and think about Him, but He also wanted me to think to Him and with Him. In other words He wanted me to direct all my thinking to Him and to be aware that He is always conscious of all my thoughts. In one of the earliest conversations, He said, *Don't leave Me in the background as a spectator. Make Me a part of all your thoughts and actions.* My first step in responding to such a plea and thus toward understanding the first lesson was to train my thoughts to stay on God.

The practice of repeating His name has been most beneficial in all my efforts to keep my mind on God. In thinking Him by thinking His name, Jesus, in two syllables over and over, I have developed the habit of synchronizing my breathing by repeating "Je" with the in breath and "sus" with the out breath. He often says, *Breathe My name deeply three times*, guiding me to do just that prior to writing or beginning other tasks and as a means to create calmness during moments of stress. I breathe His name by taking three deep breaths with the same process: "Je" (in), "sus" (out)…"Je" (in), "sus" (out)…"Je" (in), "sus" (out)…and then let the breath calmly go in and out of its own accord, saying His name with the in and out breaths naturally. "Je" (in), "sus" (out)…"Je" (in), "sus" (out), and so on. How that calms, soothes, and brings peace to my being.

Over the years the practice of mentally repeating as well as breathing His name has brought me much grace not only in stillness but also in movement, especially walking. The repetition of His name while walking has become a habit that has naturally transferred to other activities that have rhythms. I synchronize the rhythm of the two syllables of His name with the motion and sometimes with my breathing as well.

If the task at hand does not allow the synchronization of breath with repetition of His name, then whenever possible during pauses in activity, I simply try to repeat His name mentally, independent of my breathing process. Doing so, even if only briefly, brings forth a peace that has a calming effect on my body and mind and, I am convinced, holds much grace for the moment. For example, if I am sitting at the computer desk, mentally involved therein, as soon as I stand and begin walking, the repetition of His name takes over out of sheer habit. It follows that even if I do not walk at length during such a transition from one activity to the next, the habit of repeating His name grows stronger and will often take over even though I am not walking but engaged in some other activity with a one-two rhythm, and eventually to other activities with other or no rhythms at all.

Another helpful practice in the effort to keep my mind on God is mentally returning to His presence. Even if I do not feel it, I believe He is always with me, and mentally acknowledging that brings yet more grace. Of course it is most challenging to remember to return to Him in thought while in the midst of an activity. How often do I find that many hours have gone by without my remembering to direct my thoughts to Him? Thankfully, though, countless reminders of His presence constantly surround us. The wonder and beauty of nature always bring my thoughts back to Him. His desire to love us is something I am convinced is linked with all of creation. Once He told me beauty is for our pleasure and delight. He loves us in the gift of beauty, so unselfishly providing it in such profound abundance. I cannot look at a flower or a sunset without feeling gratitude, proclaiming my thanks, and praising Him for such blessings.

As I encounter people throughout the day, I talk to Him about them, asking for His blessings on them or for His help for their needs. I also thank Him for those who are dear to me. Feeling compassion for the pains and concerns of others seems to be a door to His presence. When difficult situations arise, I turn to Him in thought and ask for His help. When things are going smoothly or seem to fall into place, I see that harmony as a gift from His hands, and I thank Him. As my mind becomes occupied with associated activities, I try to bring Him into the moment and the task at hand. Directing my thoughts to Him, asking for His guidance and help, talking to Him about details as well as generalities, I find myself thinking Him more and more. Rather than wait until the day is done, if I keep returning to Him in thought all during the day, whether in breathing, walking, eating, working, interacting, observing, reflecting, recollecting, meditating, or praying, I find I am thinking of Him, or including Him in my thoughts and actions, more and more.

In spite of efforts to keep my mind on God, I often let things go around in circles in my head awhile before realizing that is what I am doing. How nice that in His kindness, He then gifts me by filling my very need to return to thinking of Him. Little hints in the guise of beauty, words, songs, and even numbers ever beckon my wandering thoughts back to Him. How sweet it is to be tickled in His playful ways whenever I suddenly perceive His hand in the many little coincidences that point to Him and the constancy of His presence.

Once, while on my way home from work, I was mulling over the events of the day, and I glanced up at the great blue sky. Immediately I remembered my desire to be in constant communication with Him. I laughed at how often I forget all about such things for a while, only to be reminded by the natural world or a loved one.

In that moment of recollection, I said aloud, "Hello!" I felt so happy, it made me laugh, so I said it again, more quietly and seriously: "Hello." What a blessed moment, but alas, after returning to the events of the day, I forgot all about that nice greeting. How many times have I left Him hanging, waiting in the background to be seen and remembered again? It's a good thing He is patient with me, but what are a few hours, days, months, or even years compared to the full awakening that will come sometime, and then eternity?

He often interrupts my thinking with a simple whispering of my name, as if He desires to remind me He is ever available to help me with anything I am doing or planning, and I need not do anything alone. He reminds me of many truths but most often of His love for me. Frequently He reads and answers my thoughts even before I form questions. Recently He called my name and said, *Notice Me, talk to Me, stay with Me.* I realized I had been trying to accomplish something on my own, and after hearing His sweet words, though I knew my folly, I felt whole rather than disconnected (as we may otherwise feel after being corrected).

Once I asked, "Are You reprimanding me?"

He said, *I am loving you, My dear.*

I felt my heart melting as I fell in love with such a wonderful one. Falling in love and being in love may so fill the heart with perceptions of the beloved that no reminders are needed, nor is any effort required to return to the lover in thought. In the state of being in love with my Lord, my thoughts turn automatically to Him like the needle of a compass ever turning north. Returning to and remaining in the loving presence of God is indeed the highest practice, the one most beneficial to keeping my mind on God so I may ever and ever think Him.

As I write, my whole being is immersed in the meaning of His words: *I am loving you.* I find such incredible sweetness with each stroke of my pen. How can it be so good? But it is. He is! I place myself at His feet in such gratitude to be so blessed. As He reveals many wonders to me, I am humbled before such awesome goodness and tremble from head to toe. As I feel more prompting to continue writing His words, the trembling increases, and I wonder what is in store. I look at all this sometimes as a spectator, and then suddenly I find myself in the middle of it all while He is looking at me. He is looking into me. He is here. He is standing in front of me, waiting so patiently for me to look up and, without a word, grasp His hand so he can lead me into the next step on this blessed path of love. Such a sweet, sweet, patient, beloved one is He, waiting for and yet all the while loving me. Oh, blessed, blessed living reality!

Chapter Two

Let my life be a prayer,
Oh my God,
A prayer for Your love
To enter the hearts of others
Through my service to them,
My love for them,
My desire for their awakening!

How can this be?
How can I make
My life like a prayer?
Show me the way,
Oh my God,

Your way,
The only way.

What is a prayer?
A call from the heart
To You, oh God,

Living Reality

To You.

A call for a need.

The greatest prayer merely
For the need of You
To be known
By the heart and soul,
For the need to love You
And know Your love.

So my life will be
A cry,
A call
Echoing from the hearts
Of my loved ones
(And others I know not)
To You, oh God.

For You to reveal Yourself
And for You to show us
How to love You.

How can my life
Be such a cry for You?

The only way
Is by constant remembrance
Of You.

In other words
Stay near You,
Stay with You
In all I think,

All I do,
All I say.

Then, in constant being
In You,
My life cries out:
In Him I live
And move
And have my being.

And the greatest need
Is fulfilled:
The need to know You,
To love You,
And be loved by You.

Today we shall begin lesson one: think Me. Clear your mind, My dear, of all but the thought of Me.

"Yes, Lord."

I can teach you more in one instant of deep meditation than in all the words in all your books. So come, My child. Come deep into My heart of love. There I will teach you all you'll ever need to know. You will know in a flash what your mind may try to figure out in hours of thought. So come in now. I have much to reveal to you and in more than just a flash.

"I come, Lord! Thank You."

My child, My dearest child. Talk to Me, and listen to Me in the silences of your heart. Then you will be certain it is I. Don't leave Me in the background as a spectator. Make Me a part of all your thoughts and actions.

"Yes, Lord."

Am I not the source of all love?

"Oh, that my love for You would come to the surface!"

Oh, that you would dive deep to find it first. You must find Me within. You must no longer look for Me without. You must find Me within. Then you will see Me everywhere! Live one day at a time. Study, exercise, concentrate, meditate. No more outer stimuli. Find Me within. You must go deeper. You must not remain on the surface. You must go deeper.

☙ ❧

Intoxicated with You,
Oh Lord,
I know not what to do.

Bubbling over and over
With the joy
Of Your nearness,
Your heartbeat,
Your love,
I cannot perform
Unless it is for You,
With You, and through You!

Lift my hands.
Move my feet.
Perform Your work
Through me,
My beloved,
My dearest,
My one!

"My Lord, when I think of You in my heartbeat, I think of You in the beat of all hearts, and I think of You in all things. How incredibly wonderful that You are everywhere, all the time! You are in the very air that surrounds me and touches my skin. You are in this air as I breathe. You are in the people I see, those I hear, and those I touch. You are in the leaves, the bark, and the very life of the trees, grass, flowers, birds, and beasts. You are in all things. All of creation is in You, and You permeate every fiber and substance of the universe, and of me! Oh, my beloved, I love You. I adore You as You touch me and hold me in all that surrounds me, in all that is within!"

All I touch is sacred, yet can you think of anything I do not touch in essence? Is not all contained in Me? Is not all in essence of Me? What appears as unsacred is so only because of unseeing. I give you sight, My dear, that you may see and know all is sacred that I touch, and if you see My touch in all, will you not then behold all as sacred?

ॐ

>Oh my God,
>How my heart
>Is expanded in love!
>How my mind soars!
>How my soul is reborn!
>
>You have new blessings
>Each day for me.
>
>When I think
>I've had my fill,
>You send me more!
>
>You do love me,
>My God,
>I know.
>
>Will You receive
>My humble gift of thanks:
>My tears?

"How can I thank You, my dearest, for all Your wondrous blessings, especially this blessing of Your presence as love? I long to give of this love to You, my Lord, for it is You. Show me how to love You with this love."

My sweet child, I am showing you how. When I prompt you to come to Me in the stillness and enter My embrace, this is how you may love Me: You love Me most when you come into Me. The more completely you come into Me, the more completely you are loving Me. You are loving Me best when you put all your being into the effort to attain complete oneness with Me, to realize complete oneness with Me. This is how I want you to love Me: give yourself to Me as completely as you may, each day, and increase your efforts each day. Increase your desire for Me as you increase your efforts. In desiring Me you are, in truth, loving Me, are you not?

"Yes, but not completely."

Precisely, My child, yet as you increase your desire, your love increases too and comes closer and closer to completion in Me. In longing for Me, you awaken yourself more and more. I receive your longings, and I reward you with more love as your capacity to receive increases. Thus will your capacity to give increase as well, and you shall give Me more love automatically as your heart grows more in love's expansion. Do you understand?

"I feel more understanding. Thank You. Never let me forget Your instructions, Your counsel."

You always have Me, dear little one. If you should forget anything at all, just ask. My dear, you can ask me anything you wish to know, and if you are ready I will answer. If you are not ready, I will guide you until you become ready. So do you see how I take care of you?

"Oh, yes, my Lord. I know You take care of me. Endless thanks. How I love and adore You!"

Keep telling Me of your love, My child. I never tire of hearing it. This too will increase your loving capacities both to give and to receive.

"Then I shall repeat, 'I love You, Lord' over and over again until the very birds will join in my song of love for You!"

They already have.

ಅಃ

Marie M. Constance

My God has revealed Himself as longing.

It is both sweet and painful.
It is the pain of love's abundance
And the pain of love's longing to fill.

As He reveals Himself thus
To my heart and soul,
I hold my friend in this.

Then, with all intentions
Held by us both
Before Him
And in Him,
I melt
Into the "yes" that is,
Knowing He is longing
For all that is
To be reunited
In Him.

This is a reality
In the now,

In the now
That knows
The longing He is,
For the knowing
He is
Until all know
The longing *is*.

When all know,
The fullness

Shall be forever.

Now, as I become
More and more immersed
In His love,
I feel His longings.
I feel His love
For me,
For my friend,
For all.

I love your littleness. Give Me your weakness. Give Me everything, My dear. Give Me all!
"Tell me what You want of me today."
Stay with Me, My dearest. Stay in Me, My love. Talk to Me. Listen for My voice. Breathe in My name. Breathe out My name. Stay in My peace, live in My love, and then, My child, radiate My joy!
"My sweet, sweet Lord, You are so wonderful to me. You are everything to me. How I love You and long to be pleasing in Your sight."
My dear little one, if you follow these, My wishes, you will always be pleasing in My sight. Yet know that even when you do not follow all I tell you to, you are still pleasing in My sight simply because I love you, and I cherish you always and forever. Realize this if you do nothing else in life: realize I love you and I long for your love. This is your main task on Earth. When you realize this, you will do My will without struggle and without fear, for so united shall we be that you will no longer say, "I long for You," but "I am in You" and "You are in me," and you will know this and live this the rest of your life.
"My dear Jesus, receive my tears as my thanks. Receive my efforts. Receive all I am, though I am so little."
Remember, I love your littleness.
"My Lord and my God! Oh, my Lord, make me ready!"
You are already ready.
"I don't feel ready, my Lord. Just look around. Where are the fruits?"

They are yet to come. Listen. Always, always listen for My voice. I shall continue to speak to you, My dear, because I have chosen you as My channel. Fear not My absence. I am and ever shall be in you and with you, and you shall ever be in Me and with Me. Listen and love. Enter and be. Live forever and ever in Me!

"I do so love and adore You."

I know this, but just as you long to hear your dearest ones tell you tenderly of their love for you, I long for you to speak this way to Me. Will you satisfy My longing, My dear? My dear, dear one?

"Oh Lord, when You speak tenderly to me, I just melt. Yes, of course I shall speak tenderly to You. Receive my every tenderness, my dearest, dearest dear."

You receive too, dear. OK?

"OK."

☙❧

> My Lord God,
> Sweetest of all!
> I am so grateful
> For this gift of Your love.
>
> All those months of waiting.
> How could I ever forget
> You?
> How could I ever forget
> How sweet is the taste
> Of Your nectar:
> Love?
>
> I adore You now.
>
> Let me stay with You awhile.
> Please keep me from slumber.

I long to be ever awake
In Your love,
In the arms
Of You,
My beloved,
My divine Lord,
Ever and ever
In You!

I have felt so very close to You
All this day.
I long to remain thus
In Your sweet presence.
(Who wouldn't always
Desire such a blissful state?)

Intoxicated
With the blissful wine
Of Your presence,
I am at Your feet.

Bless me, Lord,
And show me how to love You
With this wondrous,
Ever-flowing
Love divine!

This is how I want you to respond. Know that I am always with you in love. In every little thing you do, love Me. Think your thoughts to Me. Direct all your thinking to Me. When you find you have wandered in thought from Me, just call My name (tenderly, please). It is all so simple if you realize I am always here, in you, with you, within you, and around you. When you doubt yourself, give it to Me. When you question your actions, give the results to Me, even your little failings. When you give the results to Me, there are actually no failings. When you love, give it to Me. When you receive love, give it to Me. When you receive pleasure, give it to Me. Give all to Me, My dear. Live in Me by bringing all, by offering all, by giving all to Me in this that I am.

"Wow! If ever I have any questions, I should just turn to this page."

No, My dear, you should turn to Me.

"Yes, Lord, always and forever, yes!"

Now, let us begin another day together.

"I just remembered what You said to me earlier. I was thinking how every day is a new beginning, a new chance, a new opportunity to find You in new ways."

Yes, and I said, "All things are new in Me." Meet each day, My dear, with this thought. Great blessings flow from and through such thinking. You must attend to other things now, but we may still talk. Always talk to Me. No matter where you are or what you are doing, always talk to Me.

☙ ❧

> My Jesus,
> I think of You
> Each time I stop activity.
>
> Even during activity,
> Anything rhythmic
> (Like walking)
> Speaks Your name:
> "Je-sus, Je-sus"
> Or, "My Lord, my Lord, my God."
>
> This habit
> Of repeating Your name,
> Calling on You
> Over and over and over,
> Is truly a blessing.

Living Reality

I thank You
With all my heart and soul
For leading me
In this direction.

For no matter what else
I am about,
I am trying
To stay in touch with You.

The more I say Your name,
The more I talk to You,
The more I love You.

Even in the dark
Of doubt and confusion,
Your name
Is my guiding light.

You are so wonderful,
My dearest dear.

Take me into Your heart
And let me stay
Ever and ever in You!

It gives Me great pleasure whenever you call My name, and when you call My name in love, I bless you and those in your heart, dear little one. So you see it is all very simple. Continue to call My name in love, and great shall be My blessings upon and within you. Think Me while you are performing any action. Try to think of Me. I shall guide you in every detail of your life. If ever you should wander in thought from Me, return to Me simply by calling My name. That is all, and the more you love Me in this way, the more receptive you shall be. Do not forget I have asked you to receive not only for yourself but also for your dear ones, for all. Your receptivity is increasing, My dear. Believe this! I know you have doubted this, and what did I tell you?

"That I had judged myself not by Your standards but by man's."

And do you now see how different these standards are?

"Yes, Lord, I do."

Keep placing yourself only before Me. I shall tell you all you need to know and all you need to do to please Me. Yes, perform your daily actions, but do it all for Me, in Me, and with Me. There shall be your joy—in serving Me in all you do!

෪෫

My very heartbeat
Calls upon You.
"My…Lord,
My…Lord,
My…Lord."

My every breath
Whispers Your name.
"Je…sus,
Je…sus,
Je…sus."

My Lord,
You are my life,
My blood,
My breath,
My all!

Have I not revealed to You the key to the door of My presence?

"Yes, Lord. Your name is the key."

Yes, but at first it would not open the door. You had to mold the key to fit. How did you mold the key?

"By repeating Your name over and over and over again."
Yes, but there is one more thing.
"Repeating Your name with love."
Yes, that was My gift to you, but you responded and received. This is how you were able to mold the key!

☙❧

My Lord,
I couldn't wait
To be back here with You
In this special place
Where I might sit and relax,
Breathe in,
And breathe out,
Letting restlessness subside
And calmness settle in.

I wanted to stay here
Earlier in the day,
But You were calling me elsewhere.

Now I can stay as long as I like,
As long as I may,
Until sleep tries to take over.

You do not mind,
Do You, my Lord,
Where or when or how
I seek to be with You?

Just that I do.

Even if just for an instant

I turn my thoughts to You,

Such is Your joy:
That I should remember You,
That I should look for You
(Though You may hide so I might seek),
That I should love You!

Oh, my one,
My only one.

Forever and ever
Shall I remember
To look for
And love
You!

What matters most to Me is not what you are doing but where your heart and mind are. If you keep your mind and heart ever attuned to Mine, then you please Me greatly, for I am orphaned by so many, abandoned utterly to the tasks and demands of this world. Complete the tasks I put before you, and meet the demands that come your way but only for one reason: to do it all in awareness of Me! I am playing with you to see if you will stay with Me and remain in Me no matter what comes your way. If you play with Me too and meet the challenge to remain, then we both shall celebrate your victory. You must admit it is all very simple, yet the mind can complicate. True?

"Yes, Lord, how true."

Strive to simplify all aspects of your life in as much as balance requires. Moderation, of course, is a good check, but simplify your thinking with thoughts of Me, My will, My constancy. Give all thoughts over to Me that try to complicate. Let go and let Me.

CR ⊗

Living Reality

My heart has been lightened.

There was a weight upon it,
And now it is gone.

Joy returns, and I am sent upon
Whirling winds of happiness.

I feel His hand resting upon my heart
After His gracious gesture:
Removal of the thorn
That not only weighed upon me
But poisoned as it penetrated.

Now the antidote: joy!

Oh gracious God,
Who am I
That You should come
To rescue me?

I am inconceivably
Your child!

"Oh Jesus, thank You! Thank You for pulling out this thorn. I could not find its point of penetration, though I could feel its toxin throughout my being. Now You have removed it and all traces of its ever having been there. When You heal, it is as if there never existed anything but Your sweetness, Your fullness, You!"
Sweet child, I am all that exists. All sweetness, all fullness you may find in Me! My dear?
"Yes, my Lord?"
Are you willing to do anything for Me?

"I think I am, Lord, but You know me better than I know myself. Am I? Am I willing?"

Yes, My dear, you are, but when challenges come, the best way to remain ever willing is always to remind yourself of who I am. Then nothing can stand in your way—nothing. When you know who I am, you can do anything, and you will do anything I may ask of you.

"Jesus, what about when I forget who You are?"

Then I come, My dear. I come and I remind you, don't I?

"Oh, yes! It's almost worth it to forget so as to be reminded by You."

My precious one, how you delight Me. Come. This shall be a joyous day, a delightful day for both of us.

"Take me, Lord."

Take My hand. Come!

☙❧

> My beloved,
> Your love
> Penetrates
> So deep,
> So
> Very,
> Very
> Deep
> Into the
> Core
> Of
> My
> Being.
>
> When I follow its course,
> I travel
> As if in a dream,
> Floating,

Gliding,
Expecting,
Listening
For the tiniest sound,
Gazing at the center,
Looking
For the tiniest glimmer,
Expecting.

You are expecting too.

Waiting for me
To hear,
Waiting for me
To see,
Waiting for me
To come
To You
In total surrender,
In total submission,
In total love!

Realize that some things cannot be revealed in words. They can be felt only in the hidden depths within.
"My precious God."
Come deep, My dear."
"My Lord, tell me more."
I said you must go deeper to really to know these truths, My dear. I want you to go deep.
"I've been looking for the time to do this, as You know."
Yes, and I shall provide you with the time you need, My dear. Will you respond?
"I shall. I will respond with all I am. I shall say, 'Yes!' and follow Your lead deep into Your heart of love, where You shall instruct me more."

There will be no need for instruction, My dear. You will simply know.

"I long to please You, so let me know Your will until the time to go deep comes. Let me know what You desire of me now."

You please Me in your keeping your thoughts ever attuned to Me, My dear. You please Me in your conversing with Me about the smallest details of your life. You please Me when you include Me in all you think, all you do, all you pray. Keeping pleasing Me thus, My dear.

"Yes, Lord.

૭૩ ৪૦

Oh, intimate lover of my soul!

How sweetly You come to me.
How gently You reveal
Your presence.

I pause
Momentarily
Between actions,
And You seize
That very moment
To enter my heart!

In action
I was unaware of You,

But in the tenderness
And warmth
That swept through my heart
In such a blessed moment,
How could I not respond
With all I am:
"I love You"?

"My Lord, You are so beautiful. So unbelievably beautiful! Daily You intoxicate me with perceptions of You in all the beauty abounding. I love You, my Lord. I love You in all that is beautiful."

I am so glad you perceive Me, more and more, My child. Keep on perceiving. Keep on loving Me thus. I will keep on revealing Myself more and more until one day you shall perceive Me as I am, in all My fullness, in all My glory. This awaits you, My dear. Keep on, and someday I may grant you your deepest desire: to know Me as I am. Know that I long to reveal Myself not only to you in this way but to all My children. If only they knew. Will you help them know? Will you?

"I will do whatever You ask. Whatever You want of me, my Lord, I shall do."

That's it, My dear. That is what I long to hear, and do you know what else I long to hear?

"Tell me."

I long to hear you say My name tenderly—yes, tenderly—with all the love in your heart.

"Is there anything else?"

Yes.

"Tell me, please."

I also long to hear you talk to Me as your dearest, telling Me your deepest thoughts. I long to hear you tell Me these thoughts. So often you just think them, forgetting I am waiting for you to talk to Me. Direct your thoughts to Me!

Lesson Two: Acceptance with Humility Goes Hand in Hand with Trust

*Let peace settle upon your heart, My dear,
as you accept humbly and trust.*

Chapter Three

There is a natural progression from lesson one to lesson two. Keeping my mind on God brings such increased awareness of His presence that often my heart is sweetly enfolded in peace. Such a state is conducive to an attitude of humble acceptance and trust. I begin to relax my hold on life's events so as to allow a shift in control, letting go of my own wishes, to let God be in charge not only of the world but of me and my life.

The certainty of the seasons of the year, with their gradual and sudden changes, is a comfort to me. I am accustomed to them and even welcome them, yet in other seasons of life, though I may anticipate change, it is often not without trepidation. My Lord has a way of gently penetrating my resistance to change, diffusing my fears, and reassuring me by revealing deeper truths hidden in the simplest observations. I am reminded of a day when He interrupted my thoughts while I walked along a riverbank. As I noticed how the tide had changed, He told me, *High and low tides are natural parts of life, My dear. You will learn to accept them as you know I am with you through it all.*

His words of advice offer a good springboard for reflection on lesson two: acceptance with humility goes hand in hand with trust. Whether from my desire for or resistance to change, I have had to learn to accept humbly and trust Him. He has led me to an understanding that He is the one true constant through all change. Just as easily as I accept and look forward to the changes of the seasons, trusting in their cyclic rhythms and the promises each offers the next, I need to accept the rhythms of life with the ebb and flow of fullness, seeing changes as parts of the whole, each change holding within hidden truths yet to be revealed. Seeing the wisdom of Mother Nature and pondering her ways, I sense the wisdom of the creator and hope to learn acceptance, humbly trusting that God's way is not necessarily my way, and God's way is the best way.

Trusting in His wisdom and accepting that which comes my way while humbly realizing the limits of my understanding, I may learn the essence of a spiritual path known as "letting go and letting God." On such a path I may discover the existence of a picture much bigger than the one I am able to see and a greater vision unimpeded by the confines of narrow-mindedness. What a sense of freedom! He once told me to be rid of all preconceived notions in order to allow a broader perspective in my thoughts and perceptions of His identity. In trying to identify as well as let go of old concepts of God, I have, in a sense, opened myself up to *unlimited possibilities*. By allowing Him to expand and increase my knowledge of Him, I may better understand His relationship to me and, in turn, begin to see more clearly how I may relate to Him not only in prayer and meditation but in activity as well.

Trust nourishes my relationship with Him. So many times He has reminded me of the need to trust Him and myself, especially in times of doubt. Once I told Him I feel for all who do not know Him and complained I did not see how I was helping others feel His presence.

He replied, *Remember: Do all for Me and in Me. Do not look for results. Leave that to Me. Just remain in Me! I love you, My dear. I love all. Trust Me. I know your thoughts. I will bless all whom you bring to Me. If you see they are troubled, My dear, do not join them in their gloom. Love them and feel for them, but do not let yourself be downcast. Rather lift them, bring them in, and love them in this that I am. Let Me love them in this too. Bring all in. Bring all to Me.*

How wonderful to have my complaints turned to praise for such a realization. By letting go of results, I free myself and free Him to free and bless those I bring to Him as well.

Living Reality

Turning to Him I realize He is a builder, an up lifter, and a healer of wounds, ever helping me grow confident in His constant help and guidance and increasing my awareness of His all-pervasive, all-gracious hand. Throughout much of my life, I have struggled with self-doubt and a lack of self-confidence, yet He has often assured me that I have pleased Him and that He does not expect me always to be able to do everything perfectly. He makes me laugh at myself whenever I realize I am expecting too much of myself. For example, once I said, "I've been rereading those things You said to me last year, and I am astounded. How am I doing? The things You said were so profound, yet I feel as if I've been slipping away somehow. Help me see things once again from Your perspective. Oh Lord, tell me all I need to know!"

In that wonderful humor, He replied, *That's a tall order!* Then I felt His smile, which immediately dissolved my feelings of uncertainty.

At a time in my life when I was overwhelmed with feelings of grief, He made His presence known to me in a tangible way, giving me a sweet peace that melted away the pain of sadness. In other times of feeling regret or remorse for mistakes and misunderstandings, He counseled me so I could better understand myself and others. In such counsel I have been transformed through feelings of forgiveness and the healing of old wounds.

Once He asked me, *My dear, do you recall reading that you please Me in the struggle? Or that simply by struggling or being willing to struggle that you are pleasing Me?* When I replied that I did remember, He answered, *Don't forget it. OK?*

I thanked Him profusely and exclaimed, "How You have lightened my heart. How You have removed a burden I did not even know I was carrying. Oh, thank You. Thank You!"

I recall how happy I felt the first time He told me of His longing to love us and His longing that we let Him love us. After I had asked Him how I could thank Him for all His blessings, especially those of His presence as love, I pleaded with Him to show me how to love Him in return for all His gifts and blessings. The longing to love Him was often almost too much to bear, so great was the love I felt from Him, so strong the love

I felt for Him and desired to give to Him. Sometimes I felt as if my heart would burst! In response to my pleading, He replied that I may love Him when I come to Him in the stillness and enter His embrace.

Imagine! He wants me to allow Him to love me. He really does desire to love me. To thank Him I must do this. I must let Him love me. Contrary to my thinking that the best thanks would be to do this or that, I know now that He actually longs more for me to be than to do, because in being I am actually receiving as He wants.

Once when I complained of the pain of love's abundance, His reply was, *How do you think I feel?* That gave me a clue, but it was only a partial glimpse of His longing to love us and for us to receive him.

One morning, as I set about the usual tasks of the day, I felt His prompting to focus more within. I heard the ever so familiar, ever so endearing words, *Come in.* I decided the housework could wait as I felt that particular prompting was for stillness as well. How He flooded me as I answered His call to enter and His call to come in! He was calling me to relax, to let go of tensions, worries, fears, or anything that might block the flow of His grace, His peace, His love. In that letting go, he reminded me of the most important things in my life with and in Him. His words came back to me: *Let Me love you and bring all in this loving.* Sweetest peace permeated my entire being, and a most tender love filled my heart. Then more words surfaced from deep within my memory: *You love Me best when you let Me love you.*

Oh, how His words bring new light to the age-old question of how best to practice the art of loving God! I long to respond to such a profound yet simple truth, that I may best love awesome God by letting Him love tiny me. How may I let go and surrender to such a wondrous yet intimate request that I let Him love me and bring all in such loving? It is for me simply to marvel at first at such wonder and then proclaim, "I will! I will if you just show me, my God, how to let You love me."

Yet until He shows me, I will seek to answer my question: how? To let Him love me, I believe I must give time to quiet prayer and meditation wherein I may be free from distractions to enter His embrace. Then I will take the peace, joy, and love awakened in that quiet time into the rest of the day to meet, greet, and interact with His other children. I will cultivate an attitude of gratitude, thanking and praising Him throughout the day and night for all His gifts. Even in times of struggle, I will remember to thank Him. In such periods of trial, I may hold on to Him even more tightly than in times of joy, accepting difficulties and facing challenges while still humbly trusting in His all-knowing providence. Striving to let Him love me by allowing Him to teach me at all times, in pleasure or pain, joy or sorrow, I will remain ever grateful for His abiding love.

Once again I am mindful of the lessons found in creation. The sense of proportion we face when beholding the vastness of mountain ranges, oceans, and the moon and stars comes to mind. Contemplating the age of the Earth and the universe can bring us humbly to the sudden realization of how tiny we really are in the entire history and realm of creation. Contrary to being unimportant or insignificant to God, the creator, we are yet individually and uniquely valued beyond compare.

Consider how amazing it is! As I join the ancients in questioning what man is that God should be mindful of him, I am filled with wonder. To realize in spite of our insignificance in size compared to the universe that we are very dear to God is humbling indeed and floods my heart with gratitude!

Chapter Four

Sweet, sweet Jesus,
I feel Your sweetness
In my heart
And throughout my being.

Your peace permeates.

Amid the struggles of life.
You are the one true constant.

You are
And You remain.

You fill the empty spaces.
Truly there is no emptiness,
Only fullness.

You are in all things.
You fill the world
And its inhabitants
With Yourself.

And though You are hidden,
There is a way
To find You,
To know You,
To know not emptiness
But fullness.

The way is but one
With the goal:

You.

You are not only
The desired end.
You are the means.
You are the way!

Jesus, I feel not only
Your sweet peace.
I also feel Your love.

Oh, what a wondrous blessing
To feel Your love!

Love is such that
In knowing it,
One is in it.

Being in love
(Your love)
Is the most wonderful blessing of all!

Thank You, my Lord.
Thank You!

Acceptance with humility goes hand in hand with trust. This is lesson two, and as you trust more and more, so shall you learn to play.

"Thank You, Lord."

It is ever My pleasure to teach you, My dear little one.

"It is my pleasure to learn always and forever from You, oh You, my blessed teacher!"

Peace. Let peace settle upon your heart, My dear, as you accept humbly and trust.

"Yes, Lord. Yes!"

☙❧

My Lord,
Are You speaking to me
In these moments
Of inner stillness
When that which surrounds me
Takes a backseat
In my awareness?
When I am more attentive
To inner stirrings,
To this inward flow
Than to outer happenings?

Tonight I perceived
A sweetness within.
I guess it was
And still is
You.

Let me not deprive You,
My Lord,
By stopping now.

Let me enter into
Prayer and meditation,

To know
Beyond a doubt
You are within!

I adore You
In this sweetness of perception,
My one!

Why must you persist in separating? Be united. Be one. Do not try to separate. Integrate, My dear. There. Already you feel peace. Are you not feeling more integrated in this very moment?
"Yes, Lord, thank You."
Now ask your question again.
"Were those Your words or the work of my imagination?"
See, you must integrate your mind as well. Let Me show you how, My dear. Really all you need to do is let go of all preconceived notions, and let Me make known to you this higher state of integration of body, mind, and soul.
"Please enlighten me."
Later. For now I wish to answer your question. Yes, those were My words. Do you believe Me now?
"Yes, I do."
Trust Me! I can do all things. Listen, listen, love, love. Continue to let Me use you as I wish. Even when you do not know how I am using you, believe I am using you.
"Oh my Lord, I cry these blessed tears now because I love You, and I feel so incredibly blessed. Oh my Jesus, forgive my doubting. It's just that I feel so unworthy at times of such grace."
My dear, I chose to use you. You said, "Yes." You continue to surrender yourself to Me more and more, though I keep you in the dark about so many things. Still, do I not provide enough light to sustain you?
"Oh sweet loving Jesus, yes. Yes! A thousand times yes. Thank You. A thousand, million times, thank You.'"
A thousand, million times, you are welcome.
"You so kindly bring a chuckle to my heart, and I perceive that adored twinkle in Your eye."

That's what I want. I want you to enjoy this with Me. So many gloomy people want to be saints. The first thing an aspiring saint must do is learn how to smile and be cheerful no matter what and to enjoy this life with all the many gifts I give. You, My dear, smile often, and this pleases Me.

☙❧

My sweet one,
Do You wait
For us to come
Running
To You?
To jump upon Your lap
In joy?
In the sheer joy of being,
As a little child?

Do You also
Await our embraces
Or our reaching upward
To be embraced,
To be comforted,
To be consoled?

Do You long
To hold us
Tenderly
As a mother holds
Her fevered child,
Absorbing the heat
And pain?
Caressing
And soothing
As if to say,

"I am here.
Do not be afraid.
I will care for you"?

Yet unlike the mother,
Who may fear for her child,
You, my God, are
All knowing,
All satisfying,
All loving,
And have not fear
But eternal hope,
Eternal joy,
Eternal peace,
Eternal love.

Oh, such good, good news!

"My Lord, I think I slept too long. What a beautiful morning, and to think I was sleeping!"
You like sleep, don't you?
"Yes, but I feel guilty for indulging too long."
It's all right, My dear. I wait for you. I like to watch you sleeping. It's just like your babies. I have told you this before. Didn't you like to watch them sleep?
"Yes, I did."
So don't feel guilty. Guilt prevents My coming in and holding you. Guilt keeps you from receiving completely, My dear. So, peace. Come, talk to Me while we walk.
"You are so sweet to me."
So are you sweet to Me. Let us enjoy this sweetness, My dear. No more guilt?
"No more guilt. I love You, Lord."
I love you, dear.
"My most precious friend."

Talk to Me, your friend. Make this your occupation, My dear.
"Yes, Lord."
But you do not need your pen.
"I know."
I always guide your pen, but always do as I ask and come in first, My dear.
"Yes, Lord, always."
I need you, My dear.
"You do?"
Yes. You forget this. I need your cooperation. I need your surrender. I need your letting go and letting Me.
"I suppose I forget because it is still so amazing to me."
This is one of those preconceived notions, dear. Now I shall help you to let go of this too. Come, My dear.

☙❧

> Oh Jesus, my love,
> What can I say?
>
> I love You more
> And more
> Each day.
>
> Life with You
> Keeps getting better
> And better
> Because of Your
> Nearness,
> Your love.
>
> Repeating Your name
> All throughout the day
> Has been my salvation,
> My joy!

Living Reality

If I turn to You
In all that comes my way,
Joy or pain,
You rescue me
In both.

Immense joy carries me away.
I become lost,
Knowing not what to do.

Then You point out the way.

Confusion or pain
Impedes my spirit,
Impairs my vision.

Then You hold me,
And I melt
In Your arms.

In Your love I am whole.
Oh my God,
My all!

"Lord, I need help."
I was only waiting for you to ask.
"Please, teach me how to come to You even though I am not alone with You. Teach me how."
You come to Me each time you call My name, each time you tell Me of your love, whether it is with words or the silent adoration of your heart. Realize this: you are always with Me now. You may not always feel the same, but know we are one.
"My Lord!"
Yes, I have promised you this. Now you need to work on realizing this more completely. You have cleared a path, and now, My child, I

want you to stay on it. With each step you take, you will realize more. You take a step each time you call My name, child. Realize this! I am truly telling you all these things. I am. The reason you do not fully comprehend is you have not gone far enough on the path. But you do not need to comprehend. All you need to do is trust in Me, in My word, and stay on the path by constantly calling upon Me as you have already done. Come, child, take My hand, and I shall go with you each and every step of the way.

☙❧

You tell me not to think of time
(For time is an illusion)
But to think of now.

Now is an eternal awareness and reception
Of blissful love divine!
And a flowing out of and into
The same.

Sweet, sweet, sweet
Is this nectar, oh my God.

How I taste
Your very life!

How I feel
Your very blood
In my veins.

How I hear
Your very breath
Whispering my name.

How I breathe in
(Oh, blessed aroma!)
Your very being.

Garland of fragrant blossoms!

How I see
Your very light
Behind my eyes.

Oh, how I know
Your very love
In my soul.

Oh, how You make Yourself known
To me.

I am blessed to behold You.
I am blessed to love You.
I am blessed to be loved by You.
I am blessed to be in You.

Forever and ever am I blessed
In just one instant
Of blessed awareness,
Of blissful being,
Of sweetest union
In You,
My God.

"My Lord, I did not write all You asked yesterday."
I am not concerned with time, My dear. Your time is different from My time. You may write today. With Me, My dear, life is one continuous

day. Think not within the limitations of time. I shall teach you more of this as you become more ready. OK? You think so much in terms of time. Let us think in terms of now. What do you think of now?

"I like now. It kind of erases anxiety, which seems to come from before or beyond now. So if I live more in now, maybe I will be more able to eliminate nervousness and fear."

Good. This is what I want you to do. Try to be more and more aware of now.

"I will, but You must help me."

You already know I will, but I want you to keep asking for My help. Come to Me, and ask Me for all your needs.

"I've wanted to ask You many things but have felt unprepared to ask."

Fear not, My dear. You may ask anything you like. Haven't I told you this many times?

"Yes, Lord."

And if you are ready for the answer, I shall tell you the answer. If you are not ready, I shall wait, yet be assured I shall give you something in place of the answer to sustain you until you are ready. I never remain untouched by your prayers, your questions, and your requests. I always respond. Do you believe this?

"Yes, Lord, I do. You are so gracious."

෬෩

> Oh, precious lover of my soul!
> I care not for fortune or fame,
> Wealth,
> Power or praise.
>
> I care only for You to be
> Ever near,
> Ever dear,
> Ever here!
>
> I ask only for the grace

Living Reality

To stay close to You
So I might love You in return
For all Your love
That comes to me.

Oh, blessed, blessed one!
Never, ever leave me.
Never, ever let me leave You!
Keep me ever and ever
In the shelter
Of Your most tender,
Most sacred,
Most loving
Heart.

Do you recall My telling you never to let go of My hand? And if you were to let go, what I would do?

"Yes, Lord, I do."

That is My response to your need today. You told Me your heart is so connected in this process of sharing with others, it is hard to let go. Now I'm telling you this. To let go you must clasp My hand more tightly. Do this with your hands and your heart, My dear. Do this each time you realize you need to let go.

"Is that the need to which You have referred?"

Yes, it is, My dear. Now, grasp My hand and come!

"Yes, my Lord. Thank You for responding always to all my needs. Oh, thank You!"

It is indeed My pleasure and My delight, My dear—My pleasure to fill your needs and My delight to feel your happiness in Me. Now, come.

"Yes, Lord, always, always, always yes!"

Let Me fill all your needs, My dear. Find all you need in Me. In this fulfillment I shall bless not only you but all those in your heart. Yes, My dear, I shall multiply this fulfillment for all.

ଔଷ

Oh blessed Lord Jesus,
Your prayer for all
Believers included me,
A prayer for unity
With You in the Father.

Guide and possess me
So I learn to love more
And live in peace
With myself and with others.

Let me grow in wisdom
So I may act
In accordance with Your will.

Oh, blessed lover
Of my soul,
Awaken me in Your love!

You do not need to be together in order to know together. Yet know that I have heard your prayer. I know the same longing. I have prayed the same prayer to My Father. I know what it is to be human. My dear child, I know and understand your every longing. I long to fulfill you so that your unity may be complete, so that your joy may be complete. My dear one, I want only your happiness and your love.

"I do love You, Lord. Yet I know I can love You more. I want to love You more. Show me how."

Then come to Me, and love Me in the silence, My love. Love Me deep within. There will your love be more complete. There will you be more able to give Me your love. There will I show you how.

"Oh my Lord, take me there!"

Come, take My hand.

"Oh my Lord, be with me in my prayer."

I am your prayer.

Living Reality

☙ ❧

Blessed, blessed God.
My God.

How can this be?
This wondrous truth
I perceive
Within my entire being:

You,
God of all,
You
Love *me*?

I doubt not Your love,
Only my worthiness.

Yet in this
Is the great mystery:

You, so great,
So wonderful,
So powerful,
So beautiful
Love me,
So little,
So simple,
So weak,
So impure,

Not because of these
I see in myself
But that which You see

In me,
Your child.

Hold me,
My Father,
My Friend,
My Beloved.
My All!

"Jesus, why do I have these terrible doubts at times?"

It is because you are coming face to face with the enormity of this, and it is at times too much for your little mind—your "foolish" little mind—to handle. But your heart—your "foolish" heart, so "foolishly" in love with Me—has expanded and is not little, dear. Listen and follow your heart. Your soul knows Me. Your heart feels Me, and though your mind thinks Me, at times it cannot handle so much, so it automatically does what it does naturally. It questions. It's OK, dear. Let your mind question, and then simply let it go. Let your heart's perceptions of Me take over, and be still in this. Then let your soul's knowing come forth and proclaim: "I am He!"

"My Lord and my God!"

My precious, precious dear, come! Do not doubt the all-fulfilling nature of My love. Do not doubt the all-knowing wisdom in My love. Do not doubt I am the source of all love. I am the continuance. I am the flow.

"What am I to do, Lord? Instruct me now, for I am so drawn by Your love that I can think of nothing else and desire nothing else but to melt in the burning flames of Your love."

Then melt, My child. Melt!

☙❧

Let me tell
Again, again, and again
How wonderful
Is my God!

Living Reality

So sweetly He answers my questions.
So gently He reveals His truths.
So tenderly He bestows His blessings,
And so intimately He converses with me
In the language of love.

Intoxicated with the joy
Of His presence,
I find my heart yearning
To be ever and ever
Consumed in Him,
Melted
Beyond identity,
Into liquid love,
So I might become Him
(One with Him)
In the oneness
Of unity,
Of union with Him.

Like a candle's burning
Flame melting wax,
Liquid losing solid form,
Flowing into its holder,
The rest becoming one with
The air surrounding,

So shall I melt
By the flaming touch
Of His love—
Melt into His hands and heart
Ever holding me
As my spirit merges
With the all
That surrounds me.

Oh, beloved one,
I yearn to be thus
Melted by
And in
And with You.

Forever and ever You!

"Show me the obstacles to my becoming. Please show me what is in the way that I might thus surrender to Your will as You ask."

There are two obstacles, My child: doubt and fear. Yes, and these shall be removed both by your efforts to please Me and by My grace.

"Reveal to me that which I need to do as efforts."

Keep on, and you shall know what you need to know, to do.

"Lord, I want to ask You a question."

Then ask. Never fail to ask, My dear. I am ever waiting for You to come to Me for all your answers.

"Tell me what You meant when you told me to keep on."

By this I meant that I desire you to continue bringing your dear ones to Me. I desire your continued sharing in writing with your dear friend and with the others I show you. I desire you to keep Me ever in your thoughts. I desire you to be ever ready to follow Me wherever I should lead you, and I desire that you come to Me, let go, and receive My love as you surrender your all to Me. I desire your love, My child, and your calling My name in love. All this I ask of you when I request that you keep on.

Chapter Five

How He is loving me!
How He is revealing Himself
In ever-increasing sweetness.

He is the sweetness.
He is the tenderness.
He is the love!

Oh, intoxication divine.
This state I am in
Of continuous awareness
Of one so dear,
Of continuous perception
Of a presence so clear,
Of continuous revelation
Of a lover so near.

So near, so clear,
So dear is He.

In each day's new awakening,
He comes.
Oh, how He comes!

He comes to awaken me.
He comes to touch me.
He comes to hold me
And caress me.
He comes to love me
And receive me
Into His embrace.

Oh, blessed, blessed
Awakening.

Oh, blessed new dawning!
Each day, all day,
Each moment, all night.

Forever and ever I am His,
And He is mine!

"Jesus, my Jesus, counsel me."

My dear, sweet little one. Receive the counsel in My embrace. Receive the counsel in My love. What other counsel can you possibly desire than the all-satisfying counsel of My love?

"None is more sweet, my Lord, than Your love, therefore I shall put down my pen tonight, turn out the light, and try to let go so I may truly come to You for such blessed counsel."

Remember, do not try too hard. Relax, breathe My name, be at peace in this, and just let everything else slip away into nothingness. Then I shall be your all, child, as you have so desired. Come. Let Me be your all. Come. Let Me love you tenderly. Let Me fill you and make you My own.

"Oh my Lord, You are my all. You are my beloved. Take me now with no more waiting, no more doubting, no more fear, just You, You, You."

Living Reality

Do you think you create all this in your mind? It is I. You are in Me, and I help you in your thinking as well as in your doing, except when you block out My help by doubting yourself. If you saw how doubting truly blocks or restricts the flow, perhaps you would resist it more. Would you?

"Show me."

Imagine a restricted vessel. Such is the vessel of one who doubts. Even self-doubting causes restriction. Do you see?

"Yes, Lord, thank You."

I do not mind that you are not yet perfect or perfectly able to meet every obstacle or every struggle. It matters not. What does matter is that you let Me in to help you, to guide you, to teach you, to heal you, and to love you. Place your emphasis not on the things you have yet to conquer but on My help, My strength, My wisdom, and My love. On these you should place the most importance. Then you will not restrict the flow but open wide the portals of your heart, and oh, shall you then know My joy. Come. Receive all I have in store for you. Fear not. Doubt not. Love. Love!

"My Lord, I melt in Your counsel. I melt in Your love. You are my all!"

And you are all Mine.

ꒂ꒓

Bless all my dear ones.

Bless all these precious flowers,
My Lord.

Let them bask
In Your light
And drink their fill
From Your fountain
Of living water.

Love them,
Bless them,

Fill them
Every day.
Amen! Amen! Amen!

"My Jesus, what am I to do?"
Let go. Give it to Me. Let Me.
"Sometimes I feel as if I have let go, and then I realize I haven't. Help me, please. Oh, help me. Help the one in need. Please, Lord. Help!"
I am here. I am helping. Peace, My dear. Write that which I told you yesterday.
"Yes, Lord. As I was admiring the beauty in shell segments, You said: 'You see the beauty in parts of the whole. That is why I am able to reveal Myself to you in part until you are ready for the whole.' Is that what You meant for me to write?"
Yes, My dear. Now hear this: I love you! Never forget this most central truth. If I love you, do you suppose I will not watch over and care for those you love most?
"No. I know You do Your part always. I am just afraid I do not do mine."
Then you must trust that all I ask is for you bring to Me all your dears, and when I ask you to let go, simply place them in My hands. You do not have to stop loving. You just need to stop fearing.
"Yes, Lord. Thank You."
Now for some of that good cheer.
"Yes, Lord."
Come, My dear. I await your smile!

☙❧

Jesus,
I long.

I long for You
To make us one
So we may be one in You.

That You make us all
Whole,
Together
In You.

I want to open wide
The doors of my heart
And take them in
And hold them there
And keep them there
And love them there
With You.

"My Lord?"
Yes, My dear?
"I told You all I want is You and to please You. Then You said, 'Then you have all you want,' yet You knew I still had longings. You told me to tell You about them and that You wanted me to be light. My question is this: if I think all I want is You, but I still have other longings, then I want other than You, don't I? And my thought about my only wants wasn't true, was it? Why do I fluctuate so?"

My dear, did I not tell you I let you feel the longings and uncertainties of others in order to share in their pain, and as you then receive the only remedy (Me!) you may receive for them as well? The longings you have felt are the longings of those for whom you have been praying. My dear, trust Me. I have also told you how you are sometimes too sensitive. There is a balance in this. You connect with those for whom you pray. I let this be, My dear, for this helps them to reconnect to Me, and when you become aware of this I ask you to hold them, don't I?

"Yes, Lord, yet I wonder how it is that You ask this of me when it seems I should ask this of You for them."

But you see, this is what I am trying to teach you, My dear: how to be My presence for them, how to be My love for them, how to be My light for them, how to be whole for them in Me. Do you see?

"I'm trying, Lord. Just keep me. Hold me so even though I don't always see, I will still be."

Yes, My dear, you must always first come to Me. Come in. Be in Me, in this that I am, and then you bring them in, you hold them in this, and you receive for them as you hold them. Yes, My dear, first, always first, come to Me. Come in. Let Me love you!

"Jesus, what about when I do not realize what is going on? What about when I am not aware of this?"

Still come in. Still come, My dear, and always, when you come, you receive and always, when you receive, hold them all in this. It's just not as easy when you are not aware, is it?

"That's for certain!"

Well then, you can give Me all things that are not easy, can't you? Or let Me in. Whatever is effortless is by My grace. In whatever is not easy, you must ask for My grace, and know you are growing in the effort.

"Yes, Lord."

Always, in any efforts, think of Me. Make your effort for and in Me, and then My grace will come, and even if you are unaware of My grace, you must believe I am always with you, and I respond to your every need. This faith will be a path to Me for those in your heart's prayer too. Your effort, your faith, your willingness, your love—these are all your gifts to Me, My dear. This is how you let go and let Me: You pray, you trust, and you proceed with or without awareness of "what is going on." Do you see?

"Somewhat, yet still I feel a need to understand more. Why?"

Because I am calling you to this, My dear.

☙❧

Who am I?

Doubts creep in
To make me wonder.

Living Reality

All I believe
Is but through faith
And limited experience.

Increase my faith,
You
Who hear and answer
My prayers.

As I doubt my worth,
My eyes pause,
Then they find this paper,
And lo!
They behold my dear little child.

She now rests
(Relaxed,
Trusting),
Asleep,
Here
On my lap and shoulder.

Of one thing I am certain:
I am her mother.
I am the mother of my children.
I am the wife of my husband.

They need me.
I need them.

Perhaps the answers
To my questions
And doubts

Lie in this simple
Yet profound truth.

God has placed me
Here in this family.

This is the part
He wants me to play.

All He asks of me
Is to try my best
To play this part well
And be mindful
Of Him in the play.

Reveal to me, oh God,
Whom You are,
So I may be
More mindful of You
(Knowing You more,
I shall love You more),
Thus better able
To play this part
You have given me.

You see, My child, how you watch your little one? You watch as she goes through all her events of the day, and your heart fills up not because of what she is doing but because of who she is: your child. I watch you in the same way, only you cannot imagine how much greater is My love for you, and I love all My children thus. Know this, and live in it! Do not doubt or fear. It is the truth, the very core of your existence. I love you because of who you are: My child!

"My Lord, my all!"

Living Reality

☙❧

Why, oh why, oh Lord,
Must others be so down
On themselves?
Why, oh why
Do they refuse to see
Your smile?
Refuse to accept
Your love?
Why must they persist
In their despairing?
Their gloom?
Their sadness?
Their being so
Alone?

Why, oh why, oh Lord,
Don't my prayers
For them,
For their happiness,
For their awakenings
Into the light of Your love
Become as real for them
As they are for me?

Tell me, please.
Tell me if I may
Change my prayer,
If I may help,
If I may somehow
Make it all seem better,
Become lighter,

Become fuller
For them all!

Oh my Lord,
Receive these,
My tears for their sadness,
As my new prayer.

Receive this,
My longing for their happiness,
As You receive me.

Oh my Lord,
Make it better.
Make it lighter.
Make it fuller,
And reveal Yourself
In love.

"Almost an entire week has passed since I last wrote in this book. You have held me and carried me during this time, yet You always hold me and carry me. It's just that this time, I was more aware of Your solace because of the pain."

My dear child. My dear, dear child.

"What is it, Lord?"

You already know. I have already spoken this to you, but you may write it. Yes, write it so you may return to these, My words, in your time of need.

"Speak, Lord."

You held Me and carried Me too, child, in your letting go of resistance, and in surrendering and accepting, you bore the pain that, though you didn't know it, was also My pain. Any pain you bear of another's is also My pain. Do you understand?

"I want to, Lord. Do I?"

Living Reality

Partly. You are growing in understanding, yet did you not say that if you understood, the pain would not be pain?

"Yes, I remember saying that. Is it true?"

Somewhat, child. The pain of unknowing is often the sharpest, is it not?

"Yes, it is. Does acceptance of the unknowing teach me to trust in You?"

You know it does, My dear. You know now it does.

"Will I remember this the next time, Lord?"

Perhaps. Now you have these, My words, to help you understand, and that should lessen the pain.

"I want to say I will bear whatever pains You wish me to bear, but am I strong enough to say such a thing?"

Did I not tell you I cherish your littleness, and I am your strength in weakness?

"Yes, Lord. I just want to ask You to show me the way I am to follow You. I do not wish for pain. You know that. I want to be willing to do whatever You want of me. Just never leave me without You. Oh, how You are my all!"

I shall never leave you. Never. Now, you must attend to the children, but that does not mean this conversation should cease. Haven't I asked you to talk to Me more, no matter where you are or what you are doing?

"Yes, Lord. What do You want to talk about while I'm in the kitchen?"

Let's talk about being in Me.

"As You wish. Hold my heart."

Take My hand.

"How blessed You have made me. How blessed I am! Thank You, Lord. Thank You!"

You are welcome.

"You are so very courteous."

Imitate Me. Imitate Me in all ways, My dear. Imitate Me.

☙❦☙

Jesus…
Jesus…
I breathe in
Your name.
Your name
I breathe out.

Your name calms me
As once
During a storm
You calmed the restless sea.

In the calmness
I am still.

Still.

Awaiting Your presence,
Following Your command
To be still
And know
You are my God.

Let go of your plans, My dear. Let Me arrange things for you. Occupy your thoughts with Me. I lead you in this. I lead you into understanding when you are thinking Me. I shall make clear to you My will. You are still learning how to trust. You know I am the one who reveals. Yet when you are tempted to doubt or to think of yourself as unworthy, you must give this to Me by breathing My name and entering My peace. Even if there is a cloud covering understanding, still you must give this to Me, and look for Me in the clouds.

"Yes, Lord."

And trust that when you do understand, it is My will, and when you do not understand, it is My will as well. You are molded into My will. I never leave you, and you never leave Me. We are one. Believe this even when you do not feel it. But truly you feel it more than you do not. Is this not true?

"It is true. Thank You."

That is why it is hardest for you, My dear, when the moments of confusion come, and you do not feel it. You feel lost, don't you?

"Yes, Lord."

Trust in these, My words, My dear: I am in you. You are in Me. We are one. When uncertainty comes give it to Me in My name. All shall melt away in My name. (I have told you this before. Remember it.)

"Yes, my Lord. Thank You."

My dear, you have been struggling because of trying to please others when you should not worry about such things. You cannot please all at the same time. You need to be concerned only with pleasing Me! Haven't I repeatedly interrupted your thinking with My words of assurance that you are and have been pleasing Me?

"Yes, Lord. You have been and are ever so dear, so sweet, so assuring. Thank You."

Then relax, My dear, and rest peacefully in My arms. Drink in the sweetness of My love for you, and be at peace about your limited ways. You may not be able always to bring about the best and most pleasant outcomes in dealing with others. Imagine! You are trying to please equally and consistently when there is such inequality and inconsistency among those you are trying to please. Believe Me, My dear, I am well pleased with your efforts, and though you see them as futile, your efforts are not in vain.

"Oh, thank You for lightening my heart again!"

It is and always shall be My pleasure to lighten your heart so I may then reclaim it as My own and reclaim you as My own.

೧೮ ೮೨

My Lord,
I feel as if
You've been trying
To reveal to me this truth:

Marie M. Constance

All You want of us is our love.

You want us to open our hearts
To let You in,
So You might truly love us,
And we might truly receive
Your love.

No matter what our pasts may have been,
You love us now,
In the present.

I open my heart to You, my Jesus,
Now.

Love me as I am.
Show me how
To love You in return!

"My Lord, this that I feel, is it Your prompting? Please tell me what You want of me now."

My child, I always want your heart, your love, now, always now!

"But is there something specific You are calling me to do?"

All I am calling you to do now is love. Love Me always. Love Me as you speak in your mind and heart to Me. Love Me in your activity. In all you do, love Me! See Me and love Me in those you encounter each day, child. This is what I ask of you now. And in answer to your question about My prompting you to a specific action now, the answer is no. That which you are thinking is not that which I am asking. It is out of your desire to make things right that you feel you should go in this direction. But I am calling you instead to prayer, constant prayer. No matter what you are doing outwardly, your heart may remain in prayer. You know this. I want you to be more constant. This is what I am calling you to do. If you have concerns, bring them to My attention if you wish, yet know that I know your concerns before you tell Me, and I will help.

The message I have for you in this is if you keep these concerns before Me and trust in My care, you may be freed from their burden and thus free to be in Me more constantly, more completely. Do you understand?
"Yes, Lord, I do. Thank You."
You see how simple it all is? Stay in Me, and I will care for you and all your concerns, and I will be your guide and your strength when you need Me. Stay in Me, child. That is all I ask.
"Thank You, my beloved, my Lord, my God. Thank You!"

☙❧

>Hold me.
>Hold me, my Lord.
>Gently hold me
>In Your Heart.
>
>Open up for me
>All the stores of wonder
>As I open up for You
>All the doors
>And windows
>Of my heart.
>
>As I open up my heart,
>Oh my Lord,
>Let me enter Yours,
>Then hold me there
>Forever more!

"I wonder what You have in store for me."
What I have in store for you is love—tremendous, wondrous, all-fulfilling love!
"How might I prepare myself for what You have in store for me, my Lord?"

All you need to do, My child, is this: open your heart, talk to Me, and listen.

"Is that all?"

Yes, My child, and then let My love flow through.

"Oh my Lord, I am so blessed to be loved by You!"

All My children are so blessed. You must help them know this.

"How?"

Keep writing. Keep loving. Keep praying.

"What else, my Lord? I feel as if You were going to say, 'And…' What is it, my Lord?"

My dear child, you must love even when it hurts, even when there is pain. You must still love. You must follow My example and love no matter what comes your way.

"Sometimes it is hard, and I just want to hide. You must help me when it's hard."

My child, I am always with you. I am your help. I am the love. You must not forget I am the love you feel, and if you do not feel it then ask for it! Ask Me, and it shall be given to you. Ask Me for love, for the strength to love. If you want to hide, then hide yourself in Me. It's all right to come to Me for shelter and protection. I am eager to provide all you need. Just come to Me.

"I am drunk with Your love! Show me what to do with Your love so tremendous, so wondrous, so all fulfilling."

Love Me with this love, My child. Love Me.

Lesson Three: Remain

Remain, My child, in Me. Remain steadfast in Me.

Chapter Six

I asked my Lord, "What do You mean by remain?" The answer came as a gift suddenly one evening. My husband and I were having a discussion after finishing our supper. While he was speaking, although I was listening to all he was saying, I began thinking about the uncertainty of how long we might still have each other, well aware that either of our lives could be taken away quickly. Suddenly my Lord broke in on my thoughts and whispered, *It's all about moments, My dear.* Through His whisper He brought me to a place of stillness, and then a wave of gratitude flooded my heart as I realized His meaning in that very moment. It was an epiphany. Tears filled my eyes as I pleaded with Him not to let me forget the gift of that moment, so rich in insight and awareness.

Since then I have thought a great deal about the meaning of the gift I received in that whisper, and have tried to be more attentive to and increase my awareness of such moments. In an instant I perceived life as a gift of many moments, and in that same flash of insight I longed to open my eyes to see the true worth of such moments. Afterward I had a renewed vigor in my efforts to live in the present moment, remaining with and in Him always, ever aware of Him, ever open and ready to do His will, ever surrendered to the moment.

Though increased awareness often comes as pure gift, I may yet ask for continuous increase and respond in the fullness of gratitude, always seeking to remain in Him, with the assurance of His ever-present help and guidance. Daily He feeds me; daily He bids me, *Enter*, and though there are different degrees of response on my part, still He is constant in love. What a wonder to be so blessed! How I long to respond totally. This too, He says, shall be. Oh, glory!

He is so present and so very attentive. Yes, attentive is a good word, and sweet—always sweet, so sweetly calling me ever to remain in His constant embrace. Oh, how can it be so good? But it is. It is! (He is. He is!)

I feel He is watching over everything I do. Every detail of my day is in His watchful eye. He talks to me about little things and about big things. He often makes analogies between natural happenings and my inner life. For instance, one day, as I was watching the rain, He started talking to me by saying, *Drink in My life, My dear, as the plants drink in the rain.* I felt an increase then in the flow of His life within me. I felt akin to the plants and all of life and living things. I felt Him smiling as we watched the rain together, happily aware of nourishment being received on many levels.

Not only during waking hours but even throughout the night, I feel His presence. Sometimes I find such pleasure when I awaken in the middle of the night because He greets me so sweetly, and I feel as if I may move even closer to Him to drift peacefully back to sleep. Such blessed nights are far from restless, for even when I sleep very little I rest in Him.

My Lord's blessings are so wondrous. I feel a wave of gratitude coming over me as I realize how incredibly sweet is the feeling of holding this pen in my hand while feeling His love in my heart! I am wondering what He will reveal to me through this process of writing. It is wonderful.

He continues to bless me with almost-constant sweetness coursing through my being. Sometimes it is so intense, I almost can't stand it. I am amazed I don't actually take flight. My feet feel as if they are off the ground. As my heart melts in the sweetness, I ask, "What do You want me to do?"

I hear the same reply: *Be. Enjoy!*

This is all so incredible and unbelievable, but I have to believe. Oh, to be so blessed. I am constantly thanking, praising, and loving Him as He is constantly loving me. I am also constantly asking Him to bless my dear ones, to tenderize their hearts. I pray their hearts will be open to such sweet, sweet love.

Whenever I call His name, He answers. What a supreme blessing! When I need to know He is here, He makes Himself known. When I tell Him I love Him, He reciprocates. When I ask His blessing, I receive it. What an incredible life I lead! I need just to breathe in the sweetness of His presence for a little while, and then He will guide me in this writing.

How very precious and dear is my God. I am led into love now—oh, the sweetest love! His very hand leads me right now into the blessedness of being. Right now I come to such a place, such a state of loving. It is from this blessedness that I write. In this place, in this state of loving and being loved, I record my perceptions of one so gracious and dear, of our own dear God, our very own! A presence of peace comes over my hand, and I feel He is truly here, guiding this writing. Not that He was absent before, but the presence is more pronounced now.

Oh, to receive! I pray you who are reading this will receive that which flows now, through my pen onto this paper, through your eyes into your hearts. It is for you. It is for all. How my heart fills up with this that flows, and though it flows for others, it is for me too. What a gracious God!

I want to write more about the person I have come to know as He has revealed Himself to me through these daily communications. He is so close to me, so constant in His presence, so available, so personable, that I tend to relate to Him as more human than divine. He often begins talking to me by saying my name or finishes what He is telling me by ending with my name. I always recognize His voice. It is so gentle and clear, yet whenever I hear Him say my name, the gentleness seems to increase and is accompanied by such tenderness, more sweet and tender than any lover may ever hope to hear in a beloved's voice. He relates to me so individually, so personally, that I know without question I am loved.

Because of His constant availability, I know more of His desire to be my companion, and I know of His desire to please me. When I thank Him for this or that blessing or simply for His constancy, He frequently replies, *It is My pleasure!* He tells me, *I want your every happiness* or *It is My pleasure to delight you* and *I desire to please you.* Often He thanks me very humbly too. Imagine God thanking us!

He has at times used my roles and experiences to teach me deeper realities and has made more of His longings known to me through the very nature of the loving relationship He has cultivated with me. Just as I have longed to hold my loved ones, and just as I have longed for my babies to let me hold them closely, He has shown me that He has longed for the same from me. How He longs for us simply to let Him love us and hold us!

I feel a welling up from within in gratitude for His many, many blessings: my dear husband, the children, so many dears in both our families, and so many dears in our circle of friends. He is so good to me! I find myself pleading with Him to show me how I might truly thank Him, yet always I get the same answer: *Let Me love you. Come.*

Imagine the one who gives all the glorious beauty we behold each and every day says to us all: *Come. Let Me love you.*

Chapter Seven

My Lord,
Thank You
For Your abiding presence,
My most treasured possession
For all time.

You did say
You would be with us
Always,
Until the end of time.
(I believe You said these words to me too,
As I am one of Your followers.)

You *are* always here!
Waiting, watching, guiding.

I am such a fool
Not to look for You
Every moment of my life!

But I am yet a child

And get distracted
By the playthings in this life.

Returning to Your side
Again and again
For comfort and reassurance,
For confidence and for love.

What a wondrous truth!

You love me
As a child,
As Your child,
As I am.

Why must I always forget
All You teach me
Over and over again?

You are so patient with me,
My God,
My Father,
My Mother,
My Friend,
My Dearest,
My most Beloved of all!

I love You too,
And I promise never to give up.
I'll always keep coming back
To You
Until the day when I stay.

Remain. This, My dear, is lesson three.

"Teach me, Lord. Teach me."
Learn, my dear. Learn!
"You know my thoughts. Guide me. Always guide me to the truth. I cannot remain without knowing the truth, can I?"
My dear, My dear little one, do you suppose after all this I would lead you anywhere other than to the truth?
"No, Lord. I trust You."
Come into My heart of love, and know I am truly here with you. Know I am the one guiding you and your pen. Come.
"Yes, Lord."
My child, hold fast to your belief in Me, in My ever-present love and care. Hold fast because many events will come your way to challenge your belief. Remain, My child, in Me. Remain steadfast in Me. If you feel uncertain and weak, come to Me! Come running to Me first by calling My name. I shall be ever at your side, ever ready and eager to guide you and help you every step of the way. Be that which I have called you to become: My love, My love living in you.
"Oh my Lord, thank You for Your ever-present love. Thank You for being my guide and my strength. Show me that which I need to see and to know in order to be that of which You speak. Save me from myself."
You are safe in Me, ever safe under My wing. Come. Come into My embrace, and I shall prepare you for the challenges ahead by immersing you in the living waters of My love. Come.
"I am Yours. Immerse me!"
So be it.

☙❧

I can hardly contain my joy,
So great is this love
Within me,
My Lord,
My God,
My love!

Marie M. Constance

Yesterday,
When I saw,
When I watched
That beautiful,
Most glorious sunset,
I felt as if You were saying:

Enjoy Me
In this joy,
In this beauty,
In this love!

Oh dear, dear God,
So wonderful,
So adorable
Are You.

So breathless
Is my response to You.

Take me, my God.
Take me
Into Your heart
Now!

"Good morning, my Lord."
Good morning, My child.
"I love to awaken into the sweetness of Your presence, feeling You are here, waiting for me to awaken and greet You."
My child, I love to hear you call My name. I long for you to call My name and then listen for My voice.
"Oh my Lord, I long to please You."
Just stay in Me, and you will please Me.
"Hold me, my Lord. Hold me."

Living Reality

Receive Me, My child. Receive Me.

"Jesus, speak to me. Tell me that which You wish me to hear."

I love you, My dear. That is what I wish for you to hear. This is what I wish for you to feel, to enjoy, to know: this, My love, this, My joy, this, My sweetness. All this is for you, My dear. Receive. Live in this. Live in Me!

"Hold me in this. Forever hold me. Oh, that I might always please You. Show me the way each and every day, each and every moment. Show me the way that I might please You, oh my Lord, my dearest, sweetest, most loving one. Forever hold me!"

Come, My dear. Today you shall know My embrace, and as you constantly desire My blessings to flow to your dear ones, so they shall receive increase. As you receive increase, My dear, so shall they—all you hold in your heart before Me. In this I shall bless, and I shall call to increase. Oh, let Me love you, My dear, so in this loving, many shall receive My love. This, My dear, pleases Me: that you let Me love you, that you receive, that you love Me in return and talk to Me. I wait for you to say My name. This morning I received your call. I was delighted to hear your call. Delight Me ever!

"Yes, Lord, yes!"

Just enjoy Me, and enjoy all My gifts. Come. Receive even more from My very hand. Lighten what I carry. Take it from My hand, even if it is joy! You know how abundant joy longs to be shared, to be given. Then receive from My abundance, and relieve Me as you let Me give to you.

"How wonderfully You explain. Please continue."

As you wish. Do you see how I cannot give unless you receive? It is My nature not to force My will upon My children but to stretch out My hand, offering Myself and all My gifts. Yet I await their response. If the response is other than yes, I wait. Yet oh, the longing I have for their yeses. Know this, My longing.

☙❧

Oh blessed, blessed Jesus!
My beloved,
My one and only
Lord,

My one and only
One.

Oh, how I love You!
How I want You.
How I long
To meet You
Face to face.

Yet take away my sight
If I could but
Truly meet You
Heart to heart,
Whole heart
To holy heart,
Completely captivated,
Completely absorbed,
Completely one.

This, my Lord,
I long for.
This I live for.
This I die for.

To be
One,
Forever and ever,
One
In joy.

My Lord,
My God,
My one.

Take me.
Oh, my beloved.
Make me one!

"My Jesus?"
Yes, My child?
"You know all things, and You know my heart. You know my deepest desires. Yet I feel as if You would like me to tell You how deeply I desire to see You face to face, how deeply I desire to see You then run to You and meet Your embrace. All these things I tell You, my sweet one, my Lord, because I feel You want me to tell You."
Yes! Tell Me of your desire for Me. Tell Me of your love for Me! Talk to Me tenderly. Love Me in your words as well as in your actions and your prayers. Love Me in any and all ways you wish, My dear, precious child. Always love Me as I always love you. Forever and ever do I love you!
"And forever and ever do I wish to love You, my Lord, my life, my love, my all! How You must long to hear us tell You of our love. Oh, how this thought alone makes me never want to stop telling You over and over again of my love. Oh my Lord, I love You! I love You. I do so love You."
Thank You, My dear. Yes, you are feeling My desire to hear your words of love, just as you long to hear these same words. Yet I long to receive your silent words of love as well. Both are precious to Me.

☙❧

Your sweetness prompts me
To be still,
To adore You
In the sweetness
Of Your presence within.

Yet I am also called
To serve You in action,

To love You by serving
My family
And others along the way.

A loving combined with serving
Within, without.

Is this Your wish for me?

"I want to be Your servant."
I want you to be My friend.
"My Lord, how can I be Your friend?"
Love Me, child. Love Me in all you do.
"Almighty God! I do love You. You called me friend. How might I be a better friend to You?"
First of all, dear friend, always be honest with yourself as much as with Me. Then trust Me. Really trust Me. Realize who I am. Realize how I love you. Think of Me. Talk to Me and listen to Me. Then serve Me in others. See Me in them. See them in Me. But most of all, My dear one, love Me!
"How wonderful You are. How wonderful that You counsel me, instruct me, guide me, and love me. I want to do all this You say will help me be a better friend to You. Help me see You in others. Help me see them in You, so I may love You in them and love them in You, oh blessed, blessed lover of us all!"
Now, My child, My friend, work on realizing who I am, so you are truly aware of Me in all things.
"Jesus, awaken me!"
Arise from slumber. Open your eyes, your ears, your heart to Me! Come, My child. Come. Know Me, and enjoy Me.

☙ ❧

Oh, joy of joys!

Friendship with a soul that
Feels,
A soul that
Knows,
A soul that
Loves,
A soul that
Enjoys
You, my Lord!

There can be
No sweeter bond
Than one
That is born of You,
That grows in You,
That lives in You,
That contains You
(Or, rather, that You contain).

I love.

Thank You, my Lord,
That I may be so blessed
As to love.
It is the highest privilege!

"Lord?"
Yes, My dear one?
"I've been feeling happiness inside."

Tell Me about it.
"I know You know what it is."
Tell Me anyway.
"I've been thinking about how wonderful it is not only that You are my friend—so close, so intimate—but also that You let me be Your friend. Oh, what a blessed, blessed privilege."
Do you know why I have let you be My friend?
"Will You tell me?"
Yes. It is because I trust you, My dear, and I enjoy being with you when you talk to Me and when you treat Me as your dearest friend. That pleases Me and draws Me to you, as does your gentleness, your love, and your unwavering devotion. I know I can always count on you to listen and do as I ask of you. Do you wish to tell Me more of your happiness?
"Yes, I do. As I thought of the joy that comes from being with my friend and getting to know each other more, I thought how nice it is just to be with You and to know you better. Lord, will You someday tell me more about Yourself?"
You mean as a continuation of that conversation you started yesterday?
"Yes! I asked You what Your favorite things are, and You replied they aren't really things. Will You tell me again, so I may write them down?"
I hoped you would. They should know this too.
"They?"
Yes. Whoever reads your book.
"Oh."
Many will read what you have written and what you shall write, but let's get back to what we began yesterday. I told you I like color. And I like it when perfect strangers are bonded in helping each other or in helping another in need. I like it when walls are let down, and people actually feel their common bond of My love. I enjoy music too, you know.
"I thought so. Tell me more."

Living Reality

I enjoy laughter and eyes that smile with My tenderness. I like food that has been prepared carefully and with love. I like any service performed out of love, not duty alone.

"What else do You like, my Lord God?"

I like words that express or try to express the wordless essence that underlies this world of form. You see, I use such words, My dear, to carry the wordless when these words rise out of the wordless. I like to see My children happy and content, at peace with each other and with themselves. I like to see My children giving of themselves in new ways because this enables them to grow. Now, we shall put your pen to use elsewhere. We may continue this anytime you like. I am pleased you wanted to tell Me about your happiness inside. Come.

"Yes, my Lord. As You wish."

Chapter Eight

Such tenderness has come over my heart.
I feel quite overcome
With an outpouring of love
From my soul
Not only as I sit in prayer
But as I go about my activities.

My Lord is pouring Himself into my heart,
Yet already it is full,
And as He overflows
As love,
As joy,
I feel He seeks
Another cup
Into which He might
Continue to pour Himself
Until, again
Overflowing,
He seeks and finds
Another and another,
On and on.

Pour out Your love, my Jesus.
Pour out Your joy,
So all hearts
Might receive their fill
One by one.

Then we will know
We are truly one
In Your love,
In Your joy,
In You!

Pick up your pen, My dear.
"Yes, Lord."
I want you to write from your heart exactly what you feel. Just let it come.
"I feel warmth throughout my body, concentrated mostly in my forehead, my heart, my hands, and my feet. I feel an energy in this warmth, but it is not too much to bear. On the contrary it is very nice and grows as I dwell on it. My feet feel very light and tingly, and my hands feel the same way. My heart burns but sweetly, not painfully. My eyes feel magnetically pulled. My face feels the energy too, especially in my forehead, and it even feels circular or spiraling there. My heart has a yearning to give of that which fills it. My hands desire to hold and caress all whom my heart loves. My breathing is calm and regular. I feel like being very, very still so I might just enjoy this wondrous state as completely as I may.

"I want to thank the giver, You, by giving back. I want to love You, the giver. I want to love the one, You, from whom all this comes. I want to see You. I want to be loved by You. I want to touch and hold You. I want just to be with You and for You to hold me. I want to feel Your heartbeat, and I want to breathe the sweetness of Your breath. All this I long for as I feel this warmth spreading.

"Now I want to be quiet and stop writing, to give in silence to You, oh wonderful silent one. So I breathe in and out slowly, my being saying Your name with each breath, in and out. The two syllables fit as if made for inhaling and exhaling one each. I close my eyes and feel even more warmth in my forehead, and I look therein for Your light, but instead of seeing it, I feel it increasing, spreading, and permeating my body, my mind, and my heart. I feel called to peace."

Now, My dear, come into the peace of My presence. You may continue to write. Though normally you would put down your pen, I'm asking you to keep writing. This is what I long for all to know: this blessed peace. I am this peace for all. I want all to know I show no partiality, though it may appear some receive more than others. I am partial to all! I love all, each and every one. I am constantly surging as love, and when one channel is clogged, I must flow more through another.

I long for all to be open, to let My love surge through. Come, you who know Me. Come. Let Me love through you. What you feel filling you is My love surging and seeking to flow in all its force, to find its destination in all. I ask you for love because My love is so great for all and I long for love to encircle the Earth. I long for all who dwell in My domain to receive My love, and your love makes this possible. I cannot force My will upon you or upon them, but when you love Me, and you join Me in the loving, they may receive. This is not clear to you now, but it shall be clear later.

Now I want you to know how important it is for you simply to love. You ask in what way. I shall tell you. When you see someone in need, be it physical, emotional, or spiritual, let My love flow to that one. Do what you can to fill the needs, but first and foremost love those in need in your heart. Truly love them by remaining in this love-filled unity. The love for them will flow most naturally and most beautifully from within the depths of love in unity. When you think of others and pray for others, always, always love them first in this love that comes from your unity in Me. This is love in the highest sense. It is pure, it is divine, it is Me. Know this. Pray in this. Love in this. Live in this. Become this. Become this loving. Become this love. Become this oneness I am in all. Become one in Me. Become Me.

CR ❦ BO

Living Reality

Tears of gratitude
I lay at His feet.

Such divine sweetness
He has sent
To sustain me,

And sweetest,
Most wondrous,
Most intimate,
Most tangible,
Most wonderful:

My Lord and my God
Has called me
By name!

My beloved
Has uttered
My name.

All ground you tread with Me is sacred, My child. Realize I truly am here. I truly am speaking to you. I truly am. Forever and ever, I am.
"My Lord and my God!"
Stay close to Me. Stay in Me. I want you near Me. I want your love, dear sweet one, Marie.
"My name, Lord, You used my name!"
Why not? Does this convince you it is truly Me? I long to convince you once and for all.
"Convince me now, Lord. Convince me!"
So I shall, but you must do your part.
"To stay in touch with You?"
Yes, and love Me tenderly. Make Me your deepest reality. Know Me. Love Me, and forever and ever we shall be one.

"I feel like dancing for joy!"
Let us then dance together, you and I, and never stop dancing in spirit. Let Me lift your heart. Let Me erase all your fears. Let Me give all that I wish to give to you, My dear. Let Me love You.
"I am all Yours, my beloved, my sweet, sweet one."
My dear, My dear little one.
"Oh my Lord, receive my tears. Receive me!"

☙❧

Inconceivable is this,
Your vast, immense love!

Pour Your love,
Oh my God,
On Your children.

Let my prayer
Break the wall
That separates them
From You,
Oh beloved
Of us all.

Our source of
All happiness,
All truth,
All goodness
And love!

"Jesus, guide me in these prayers for one in need of Your consolation and Your loving presence."
I am leading you into this praying. Be at peace, My child. Remember what I have already revealed to you, and continue to be My channel.

Living Reality

"What a blessed, blessed privilege. Thank You!"
Thank you, My child.
"It is always so unbelievable when You say that, my Lord."
Sometimes it is just as unbelievable that you say certain things to Me. I wish more of My children would talk to Me as you do, as intimately as you do. Many do, but so many, many more do not.
"Let me make up for this lack and love You more and more, my Lord, my loving Lord."
You already do this, My dear one. Now, back to your prayer.
"I love You, Lord."
I love you, child.

☙❧

As soon as my heart
Turns to greet You,
My beloved Lord,
Such joy flows through my being!

I am uplifted.
I am at peace.
I am in such blessed,
Blessed comfort.

Oh my Lord,
I keep saying the same things
Over and over
To You.

I long for my loved ones
To know this comfort,
This consolation,
This joy
As I know and enjoy it.

Won't You please
Show me the way
To help them find You too?

Won't You enlighten me
In this matter
I bring to Your attention
Day after day,
Night after night?

Patience, My child
Is what I seem to hear—
Or is it, *Persevere*?

Oh my Lord,
Stay with me,
Guide me,
Teach me,
Love me!

Let go of all that. Live in the present moment. Live in Me! I want you to write now, My dear, because I have something to tell you.

"Yes, Lord."

First of all, My dear, do you see how peaceful and harmonious your life is when you live in the peace of the present moment, giving all to Me?

"Yes, Lord. The peace is so sweet, so renewing."

Yes, and I call you to remain in this peace, My dear. You can tell when your mind is unsettled, and when you try to figure it all out your peace is disturbed. This is part of lesson one and part of lesson two. If you are thinking Me, you try less to figure it out, do you not?

"Yes, Lord."

And when you humbly accept what comes your way, you are trusting in Me, and you realize who I am. Then, even in the midst of uncertainty, you may remain in peace. Do you see?

"Do I, Lord?"

Living Reality

Somewhat, but you are still learning. These lessons shall continue, My dear, and each shall flow into the next, but each shall also continue. You see how lesson one, think Me, enters into lesson two, acceptance with humility goes hand in hand with trust?

"Yes, Lord, I see this."

Then continue in this, My dear little one, My dear Marie.

"When You say my name, my heart melts!"

When you say My name, My heart is yours.

"Then I shall never stop saying Your name, and Your heart shall be forever and ever mine, oh my Jesus, my love."

And if you listen, you shall hear Me calling your name, and your heart shall be forever and ever melted in Mine.

"My sweet, sweet Lord. Oh, how I love You."

I know. Now, let us begin this glorious day moment to moment, heart in heart, in peace. If you follow My instructions in these lessons, My dear, many shall be the blessings that flow forth in this peace through you, for I repeat that you are My channel, and so shall My will find fulfillment in you.

"How wonderful! Forever lead us into Your truth, Your way, Your light, Your love."

I am the truth. I am the way. I am the light. I am the love. I am truth. I am light. I am love! Know Me thus. Live in Me thus. Love in Me thus. Love Me.

ଓଃଚ

Oh, happy existence
In and with my Lord!

Oh, wondrous love
Penetrating deep
Yet flowing out.

Holding me
Yet bidding me
Go out

Then bidding me
Return.

Come in.

Out or in,
I am always
In
Him!

Are you ready now?
"Am I, Lord?"
You have been ready, My dear. The question now is, are you willing?
"I want to be willing to do whatever it is You desire."
Then proceed, but first, My dear, do as I have told you to do many, many times. Come in, enter, receive, know, be. Do all this, first, My dear little willing one.
"Yes, Lord. Oh, how I love You!"
This, My dear, your love for Me, makes you both ready and willing. It always has been and always will be the key.
"The key?"
Yes, the key to the door of My heart, which contains My light, My joy, My peace, My wisdom, My truth, and My love. Yes, you have always held the key to My heart, My dear little one, in your heart. Now, I want you to see this key, to receive knowledge of this key's being constantly available to you, to hold this key, My sweet one, and to use this key. Yes, My dear, I desire you to use this key now, every day of your life in Me, always. So come, My dear. I desire to feel your placing this key in My heart. Love Me, My dear. Love Me as I love you. That is all you need to know, all you need to understand, all you need to make you ready and willing. Love Me as I love you. Come, now. Come.
"With pleasure, My dear, loving Lord, my sweet, most tender one. I come!"

CB ED

I need to go into seclusion
For a day or so
To adore,
To be,
To love.

I surrender to You,
My Lord,
This wish
To be alone with You.

Soon…

Until then
Use me.
Show me the way
Lest I collapse
From Your great,
Overwhelming love!

I fulfill all My promises. Know My promises, and know their fulfillment.
"Reveal Yourself that I might know You!"
Come to Me, child. Come.
"Jesus, I love You. Oh, how I love You."
I know how you have longed to find time to be alone with Me, child, and I have watched how you have let yourself be present to your dear ones. Now we are alone, and I know you long to come to Me. Know this: you may come to Me at all times. You do not need to wait until you are alone with Me. Always come to Me when you call My name. You have made a clear path for yourself by repeating My name and by telling Me of your love. The path is clear, My child. Come.
"Why do I feel there are still obstacles?"
Because, as you have said before, you feel I am too good to be true, but I am true! True to all My promises. Come, I repeat. The path is clear.

I try to hide myself,
But my heart
Is laid bare.

I try to contain this love,
But it fills me
And lifts me
So high above this Earth.

What do You want of me,
My Jesus,
My beloved?

Teach me
How to respond
To Your ever-living
Love divine!

"My Lord, thank You for using me. It is such a blessed privilege."
My child, you are a part of Me. I use Myself in you. I am in you. I am the very life you feel inside you. Know this. I am the coursing in your veins. I am the sweetness in your heart. I am the taste in your mouth. I am the beat of your heart. I am the intelligence in your mind. I am the energy in your entire body. I am the very core of your being. I want you to know and understand this. Until you do you will not be able to truly do what I want you to do or be what I want you to be.

"Teach me, Lord. Awaken me!"
You are in the process of awakening, My dear. As I said, you take a step each time you call My name and tell Me of your love.

"Is 'the path' the path of awakening?"
Yes, and what joy awaits you. What joy awaits you!

"My Lord, My life, I am Yours. Lead me."

Living Reality

Walk with Me. But first enter My embrace while we are alone.
"Is there anything else You wish me to write now?"
No, My dear. Now you may simply put down your pen.

଒୪

God, bless my little ones,
For You have placed them in my care.

Teach me how to nurture them
And raise them
In a balanced life.

It is hard to be constant,
To be consistent
In their training.

If ever I should falter
In example
(As I do),
Let it not be
In the manners of love
But in some lesser subject.

Guide me as their mother
And friend,
Oh blessed Mother divine
And wondrous friend of friends!

Bless them and protect them
Each and every day.

Grant me the wisdom
And the love

To raise them as Your own,
Oh wondrous, ever-living God above!

"Good morning, my Lord."
Good morning, My child.
"It is a good morning, a beautiful morning."
Every morning can be beautiful, My child. Every day, every moment, if You live in Me. Let us finish this today, My dear, and then let us see what is next, OK?
"You hardly ever say OK."
Why should I not use your idioms? Do you not feel closer to Me when I speak in your own usage?
"Yes, Lord. You are more touchable."
Good. I want to be touchable. I want to be closer to you. I want your touch just as you want My touch. Do you believe Me?
"It just seems funny that You, God and Lord of all, should want my touch, little insignificant creature that I am."
Do you not delight in the sweet touches of your children? Are they ever insignificant to you? Think, then, of My loving your littleness, loving your touches as a dear mother or father delights in those of their children. Please, My dear, I do delight in you and many, many times more than you do in your own little ones. Please, believe. Please, come to Me so you will know how tenderly I love you.
"Oh my sweet Lord! Receive me. Receive my loving touch, and receive all that I am!"
Come. Receive Me. In this you shall know.
"I love You, Lord."
I know. I want you to dive into My smile. Be refreshed and swim in the happiness I wish to bestow on you, My dear, happy child. You are happy when your children are happy and filled with laughter. See how it pleases you. So do you please Me, My child, when you are happy and filled with laughter. You want to please Me? Then enjoy all My gifts, and in your happiness others will catch some of My joy.
"Please remind me of this whenever I slip into sullen moods for trivial reasons."

I will. Do not fear. You have come this far. I will keep reminding you as long as you listen.

"Thank You, my Lord. Thank You for everything!"

ଓଶ

Daily I seek
To hold You in my heart,
My Lord,
Yet countless distractions
Come my way.

My thoughts turn away
From You
And go elsewhere—
Nowhere!
I am nowhere
Without You.

When I return
To find You waiting,
I chastise myself
For leaving You,
For forgetting You.

I will keep trying,
My Lord,
My dearest Lord.

Trying
To keep my thoughts on You,
My heart with You,
My soul attuned
To You.

You are the most
Desired
Of all my desires.

Oh, that all desires
Would melt away
In the one
Great, burning desire
For You alone!

You, my Lord.
Just You.

You and I
Alone.
One.
Just one.

"Jesus, my Lord, what would You have me write?"
Only that I await your call. Why wait to ask Me for anything? Have I not told you that you may ask Me anything? Ask for all your needs. Come to Me for all you need. Is it guidance you wish for now? Then, My little lost one, ask Me to guide you when you feel even the slightest distance between us. Ask, and I shall be at your side, ready to bestow the very need for which you ask.

"I forget that You are so incredibly all satisfying. I forget that it is not Your will that I try so hard. Rather you will me to let go, enter, and receive. Then, and only then, can I proceed with You, with Your hand in mine."

Forget only that you were ever away from Me. Forget not that I desire your every happiness, My dear, dear child.

"My Lord, my Lord, my Lord. Jesus, I am calling Your name now."
My tender, loving child.

"My tender-hearted Lord. Oh my Lord, show me the way."
My sweet, sweet child, just keep calling Me. I will not let you fall. I will hold you and keep you ever sheltered under My wing. Keep on listening

Living Reality

with all your heart and mind. I will be waiting for you if your thoughts should wander. My dear little one, remember what I told you last night?
   "Do You mean about having fun?"
   Yes, My child. I want you to have some fun. Relax and enjoy Me and all My gifts. When you need to be serious, I will not fail to let you know. Now, My child, receive My joy. Be of good cheer!

⊗

Oh, sweet pains
Of Thy piercing arrow!

Stay, oh stay
Sweet beloved mine.

Yet upon entering,
Thy arrow
Dost intoxicate me so,
Continuing,
Staying.

How sweet.

My life's blood
Dripping.

Thy arrow removed.

Thy love divine
Hast touched mine.

Pierce remain
Or sweet refrain—
It matters not.

We are ever one
Wrapped in love,
Thine in mine,
Mine in Thine,
Forever one.

Forever one.

My precious child, I want nothing to disturb this inner communion we share. Nothing. If anything comes that causes disturbance, give it to Me immediately. In order for you to come deeper into My will for you, you must learn how to do this. I shall help you, but your part is your part, is it not?

"Tell me again, Lord, what my part is."

Your part, My dear, is to remain. Strive to be in My constant presence. The key is to let go. Let things come, yet give them to Me. Give all things over to Me. All you think, all you say, all you do, all you pray—give it all to Me!

Lesson Four: Receive and Be Open

*Receive and be open, My dear,
so My love will flow through,
My words will be heard,
and My word will be known.*

Chapter Nine

Receptivity may well be considered a cornerstone of spiritual life, especially if reinforced by a willing openness that allows the flow of God's grace to continue into the world. While pleading with my Lord to show me what He wants me to do for Him, I discover in lesson four that His answer lies simply in receiving and being open to His love. In one moment He tells me very sweetly and intimately that I please Him when I receive, and in the next He profoundly exclaims, *Oh, how this world needs receivers!*

Though we are very familiar with God's call to be givers in this life, we may not be as accustomed to His plea to be receivers. Perhaps giving and receiving are two sides of the same coin of offering we may make to God. As I ponder how lesson four applies to my daily life, I sense He wants me to try to keep a receptive heart not only as I come to Him in prayer and meditation but also while staying in His presence in the midst of activity. He wants me to remain open so no matter where I am or what I am doing, His love will flow through my heart to others. Then they may also receive from Him through His very words found in these writings and expressed in my life.

I understand that the idea of my Lord's giving me loving guidance in the form of words may seem quite implausible. That said, let me explain how I have come to believe He is the one conversing with me. In the beginning I often doubted I could be so blessed as to hear the voice of God, yet as the conversations became more frequent, the intervals between my periods of doubt grew longer. He often talked to me about my falling into doubt. Once He asked me to record particular experiences where I could not possibly question the reality of His communicating to me through words. Later, in times of uncertainty, I found such sweet reassurance in my written accounts of hearing His voice.

His presence reveals who is behind the voice and is, above all, the most-convincing and effective cure for doubt. In that presence I feel almost as if I am lifted out of one level of being into another. Awareness and sensitivity increase, as does appreciation and gratitude. *Tenderness* and *sweetness* are two words that always come to mind whenever I try to describe His presence. The sense of another person's being right here with me is very intense. This other person is not only beside me and on all sides but also in me and around me, enveloping me and holding me. As I feel waves of peace, happiness, and love come over me, I know it is my loving God. I know He is reminding me of His presence and the constancy of His love.

Though there are varying degrees of intensity in feeling His presence, I always know He is with me. I am so in love with this other person, whom I call by name—Jesus—and who calls me by name often now. How my heart melts to hear the voice of my loving Lord saying my name! Oh blessed, blissful love. Sometimes this burning love is so strong, I feel my heart may burst into flames.

There seems to be both giving and receiving at once. He is loving me, and I am receiving. I am loving Him, and He is receiving. At times there is no distinction between the giving and the receiving or the giver and the receiver. What a sense of oneness He has given me! Oh, how I melt now simply in the memory of that blessed state of being. How I soar too, and seem to be flying though my feet are still touching the floor. Sometimes the love is so intense, I become like jelly, and I feel as if could turn into liquid love. I feel quite drunk from it; my heart seems to be made of warm wine.

All these feelings and perceptions are, without a doubt, of and from my God. These are the happiest and most wonderful feelings, and they convince me of the presence of my God. Sometimes I feel pulled to stillness and quiet in these happy feelings. At other times I feel pulled to write, to create something, to share with someone dear the intense joy I feel, or to do something thoughtful for someone. The happiness seems meant not merely for me but for all. Often He tells me, *Receive for all*, and, *Hold all in this*. I feel so blessed to do as He says, and I feel certain He is truly blessing whomever I bring into this state of love, of loving and being loved. When I say "bring into," I mean in prayer. Sometimes, by His prompting, I visualize the entire world with His hands holding it and all in it, or I feel this entire Earth in my heart, and He tells me He blesses all in this world as I hold them thus, in this love that fills me to overflowing. And oh, how it does overflow!

Once, when I was holding one of my children, I heard the most wonderful invitation: *Come, and I will receive you, and you will receive Me!* While I was waiting for my little one to go to bed, I felt I was already with Him. How I trembled as divine energy tingled throughout my being, tenderizing my heart and melting my soul. I felt as if He were already receiving me and I Him, yet the invitation implied there was more in store for me that night. What a wonder to be so completely taken by one so dear, so intimately tender, so sweet, so intensely loving as my divine beloved. Oh, blessed, blessed life. Oh, blessed, blessed love divine. Oh, precious, precious, sweet, sweet adored one: my God, my God, my God!

After my treasured child, my little gift of God, had fallen asleep on my heart, I thought, *Now I'll stay right here and be still, here with her and Him, with no need to go anywhere else, for I may come to Him right here and now.* Oh, the tenderness that enveloped my heart as it flowed into my little one. Tears flowed—tears so sweet, of gratitude, joy, and tender love. I prayed, "Oh my God, my beloved God, show me the way in."

One night I felt such an intimate knowing of His person, of whom I'd had perceptions, little glimpses, and parts of a whole, some more complete than others. But that night it was even more intimate, more personal, and more human. How sweet, how very, very sweet! I perceived and felt a wave of bliss, yet more than a wave, there was a flowing, a filling, a penetrating, and a permeating. Yes! A permeating from within outward and from without inward, and a tenderness melting me, a gentleness caressing me, and a lover loving me! As all this blessedness overcame me, I heard Him say ever so sweetly, *I am here. I am truly here. Though you cannot see Me, I am here. And someday, My dear, you will see Me.* Tears then began to flow. How can one person be so blessed as I have been, as I am? I melt in love; I melt in gratitude; I melt in awe.

He has said to me: *The highest service you can do for mankind, Marie, is to hold them all in this that I am!* Daily He asks me to hold all, yet now He tells me it is the highest service I can do. In spite of all my fears and all my wondering if I'm doing enough, or if I'm pleasing Him, so quietly does He enter my heart and whisper my name, and then He speaks of serving mankind.

How blessed He has made me! How blessed He has made us all. Oh, how wonderful this is. While I write, an extreme tenderness comes over my heart that almost brings a sense of intoxication, but not from drink. In it my senses are keener, my mind is clearer, and my awareness of the intricacies of life increase. Sensitivities to what is underlying the surface also seem to increase.

My desire is to please Him in all I do, especially in writing as He requests. Though I am content, a longing comes to my heart that replaces the contentedness, so I long to be whole and completely satiated with the love and person of my God. He is here in me, and I am in Him, yet the wholeness is yet to be realized. I feel as if He is truly pulling me to this. I believe that my longing pleases Him greatly, and He longs even more than I do for this wholeness to be realized. As I write I approach the place where I shall enter into fullness more and more. He is blessing me and drawing me (and anyone reading this) closer and closer, and after I finish writing He will draw me unto Himself.

Oh, blessed, blessed being in love divine! Tears are returning now, such sweet, sweet tears of longing to love and be loved completely, yet with the blessed hope that such longing shall be fulfilled.

Chapter Ten

Blessed, blessed God!

What can I do for You?
What do You want of me?

You take my heart.
You inflame it.
I cannot determine
Where or when or what
I should do.

I am melted
In these fires.

If You do not help me,
I will keep falling.

My knees are so weak,
For Your love
Is so strong.

Rescue me, my Lord!

What do you hear?
"I'm listening to the sound of the wind. You were silent at first, so I turned my listening to the sound of the wind."
You have compared the wind to My breath, have you not?
"Yes, Lord. I have called it the breath-breeze, meaning the feeling of flowing breezes within. I cannot see You, but I feel You like the wind."
Do you feel My breath?
"Do I, Lord? Is that what I feel?"
Sometimes you feel a wave permeating your being, and you sense My presence in this, My love in this. It is Me. I am breathing life into you, the breath of life. When you feel this wave, this blessing, this breathing, realize it is Me. Realize I am blessing you. I am loving you. I am sending My Spirit through you.
"I am in awe that You should describe all this to me. How shall I respond to You in this blessing? Tell me, please, how I should be gracious in my response to You."
Just receive, My dear, and realize, and let this be. I want to bless you in this way more and more. This shall not only flow in and through you for your well-being; it shall also be for the good of all, My dear. Believe this.
"I'm trying. Help me see and understand."
Just believe, My dear. When you believe this because I say it is so, you please Me. You do not doubt My presence, for you feel it. Believe just as soundly in My words. When I tell you I am blessing all through you, I want you to believe and rejoice!
"Yes, Lord. Thank You. Oh, thank You."
It is truly My pleasure. I have so much to give, and how you please Me when you receive.

"I want always to receive so as always to please You. Lord?"
Yes?
"Does my receptivity cause increase for others to receive too?"
Yes, My dear. I have told you this. You always look for ways to do something with My grace and My gifts. What you are to do now is receive. Receive for all!
"Yes, Lord."
And be open, for you are doing great things by being open, by letting My blessings flow through to others, by being My channel. We shall flood them together, My dear. The great flood shall be in spirit and shall fill the Earth with goodness.
"Again You overwhelm me!"
Peace, My dear. All you need to do, I repeat, is receive and be open. This, My dear, is lesson four and continues out of lessons one, two, and three. Receive and be open, My dear.
"Yes, Lord."
So My love will flow through…
"Yes, Lord."
My words will be heard…
"Yes, Lord."
And My word will be known.
"Yes, Lord."

෪෮

    I am
    Passionately
    In love
    With my God!

    I cannot rest
    Until I am resting in His arms,
    Until I enter His embrace
    And remain.

Marie M. Constance

I am ever restless
Unless resting
In Him,

Ever divided
Until united
In Him,

Ever scattered
Until one
In Him.

With all I am,
I desire all of Him.
With all my heart,
I long to know
All that He is.
With all my soul,
I long to be,

To be His
Until
My God is my own.

Oh, Marie, simply receive!
"My sweet, sweet Lord. How tender Your love, oh, how very, very tender Your presence. How sweet, how intimate, how personal You are. Tears well up from within in response to Your gentle touch, Your tender caress! Oh, how I feel Your hand on my heart. Daily I plead for You to reveal Yourself to my dear ones, my dearest dears, and to let them feel Your hand on their hearts, and what do You do? You turn and give these very things to me, oh blessed, blessed lover of my heart and soul. Oh blessed, blessed Jesus, my love, my life, my all!"

Come. Come here to Me, My child. Come here. Let Me hold you. Don't you know I long to give these things to you? Don't you know I am revealing Myself to you in this way for you? I reveal Myself to them too but in ways that are particularly unique and special to them. This, My dear, is for you. Won't you just receive all this I wish to give you? Won't you just receive because I want you to?

"Oh my sweet Lord, what can I say as I melt into the sweetness of Your loving embrace? What can I say other than 'take me, I am Yours'? I love and adore You, my Lord. Forever and ever, You!"

And this I long to hear you tell Me. There is nothing I long for more than your love, sweet one. Realize this, and be My beloved now, each moment.

"Take me and hold me each moment. I am Yours. Reveal Yourself and receive me."

Come.

☙❧

> Forever do I plead
> With You, my Lord,
> For the happiness and peace
> Of my loved ones.
>
> Manifest Your love
> So sweet
> In their hearts and souls.
>
> This love that comes
> From You to me,
> Oh Lord,
> Let it be ever
> Channeled to them
> So we may share
> A blessed unity

In You
Now and forever.
Amen!

"The flute, Lord. Is it Your voice?"

I speak through many instruments. You need only attune yourself to hear Me.

"The world is constantly expressing You. You are in everything, and You are surging through wherever there is an opening."

Yes, and do you see why I want you not to let anything block the flow? You must do all that is within your power to keep the flow going. See Me, and let Me flow through! Do not hinder Me with worry or self-doubts. Know My love. Know Me.

"What do You want me to write?"

This: You must not doubt the reality of My communicating to you in this way. Even if you are faced with the doubts of others, you know. You could not begin to explain or convince another. The reality, the knowledge, comes from Me. When I want this to become knowledge to another, I give the gift of understanding, yet that one must be ready, willing, and receptive. Your prayers, My dear one, help Me. It is true that prayer may actually increase another's receptivity. Believe this while you pray. Believe I am blessing those for whom you pray, and if you come to Me first and then pray for them, you are then praying hard. Do you see?

"Make me see! Give me sight. I want to see and understand all You wish to reveal to me."

The more you come to Me, the more you will see and understand. Always, always come to Me.

"My dear Lord, is there anything else You want me to write now?"

I love you tenderly. I'm especially present now because it is My will to bless those near and dear to you who are in need of My consolation, My peace, My love. Stay ever so close to Me. Keep thinking of Me as the comforter supreme. Keep loving Me by letting Me hold you. Know I long thus to fill you and overflow into those who need Me even more. You have

Me. You know Me. Now, open your heart so I may make you My own and channel My blessings through you. Open and receive!

☙ ❧

Oh my Lord,
Let my prayers
For the hearts of my dear ones
Fan the embers
That lie waiting
To be stirred,
Increasing their glow
Until suddenly
They burst into flame,
One great burning flame
Of love
For You, my sweet one,
You!

Receive not My admonishment but My love! You must know I am and I love, therefore I am love.

"I love You dearly, my Lord. Bless me with awareness of Your presence. Make me Your channel of love. My heart is so full of love. I pray Your gift will not be in vain."

Just receive My love, My child. That is all I ask.

"Fill them all! Bless, hold, keep, and love them all."

I am. My dear?

"Yes, Lord?"

You hold them too.

"Yes, Lord."

And love them.

"Yes, Lord."

And bring them to Me and in Me.

"Yes, Lord."
My dear?
"Yes, Lord?"
Thank You.
"Oh Jesus, I melt in Your sweetness."
Keep on melting in Me until only I remain. You and Me: one. I await this, My dear. You can give this to Me. I desire our oneness more than anything. Give Me this oneness.
"I thought You give the oneness."
Yes, but your part is to enter and receive so I may give to you. That is how you give Me that which I desire. By receiving, you give. By giving, you receive.
"I love You, my Lord."
Come. Now let us become that which we both desire: one.
"You already are one, aren't You?"
Yes. So are you, but you must realize this. Awaken into oneness. Awaken into Me. Realize Me! Realize you. Realize we are one and always have been and always will be. Realize and be.
"Yes, my Jesus. Yes!"
Come. Put away your pen.
"Yes, my Lord, my God, my one."
Stop writing, My child, and give yourself to Me now.

ଓଃ৪ଠ

>Oh, my beloved,
>Show me how
>To receive You
>And Your love!
>
>If You want me
>To receive,
>You must
>Show me the way.

You must reveal
To me
The secret
Of opening up
My heart,
My soul
Completely
To You!

"My Lord, I feel as if You are challenging me but freeing me as well."
I am loving you, My dear. Realize this if you realize nothing else: I am forever loving you. Receive. Receive. Oh, how this world needs receivers! So much depends on this, My dear, and I am counting on you to realize this and remain in My love so you may be the world's receiver. Do you recall My words about multiplying?
"Yes, Lord."
Realize I can and will multiply this. I am this love. This love I give. Myself I give to all! If only all would receive. My dear little one, if you receive, I shall let you receive for all. I shall multiply the receiving. Do not doubt My will. Just accept My will, and believe My will, and do as I ask: Receive! Come, My dear. I await you. Let Me love you more.
"My Jesus."
My dear Marie, precious beloved, come!
"Yes, Lord. Always, always: Yes! Yes! Yes!"

☙ ❧

It is as if my Lord has formed
A long, sharp sword
Out of His love
And, as He reaches out,
Extending this sword
To give love to another,
He pierces me.

Marie M. Constance

This sword goes right through me,
And the pain is so sweet,
So desirable.

But it is pain.

(Another paradox
Of inner perception.)

Why pain?
I do not know
Unless
It is the incompleteness
That makes for pain.

(This is a thought to be pondered.)

Union, wholeness, makes for bliss.
Desire for union makes for pain.

I am certain of this:

This is love.
It is from Him.
It is for Him.

I must fall on my knees
In awe of His ways,
In humble acceptance of His will,
In surrender to His love,
Intoxicated by His presence!

Oh, how my soul adores one so sweet—
My Lord and my God!

"Oh my Lord, how can there be more? But You keep on increasing this divine bliss within. I am drunk with love! I am melting in this liquid love divine. Use me, Lord. Oh, use me. I feel as if I'm just being. I'm not doing, I'm just being. Use me somehow, oh please, for the good of all!"

I am, My dear. I am. By just being, you are allowing Me to use you. Do you see?

"Oh Lord, I only feel now. I feel so blessed."

You feel Me! Receive, My dear. Receive.

"Is that what I'm doing? Receiving?"

Yes, My dear. By being in this, by being in love, by being in Me, you are doing the highest action. You are receiving Me for all.

"Oh Jesus, I melt. I cannot even write any more."

Then put away your pen and do My will. Be in Me!

"Yes, Lord. I worship You, I adore You, and oh, how I love You."

This I melt in, My dear. Come, let us melt together in this being. Oh My dear one, come!

"Yes, Lord, yes. Oh divine ecstasy in You. You! Oh Jesus, Jesus, Jesus. How my hands and feet are burning with Your love. Yes, that's what I feel. Light energy is truly love. How I am in love with You, my God, my love, my beloved. You! Oh, to be so blessed by love! Oh my Jesus, my divine lover forever. All I can do is exclaim and proclaim that You are love. And all the while, I am melting in liquid love divine. Forever do I plead with You, oh God of all. Fill all with this love I feel, this love that You are. Oh my God, fill all!"

My precious dear, I am filling all as I fill you. And as you bring all to Me, so do all become filled as you are filled. Oh, My blessed, blessed child, receive. Receive! Receive for Me; receive for you. Receive for your dear ones. Receive for all!

"Oh my Jesus, my love."

Oh, My Marie, My dear. Always, always, always dear. Now, My precious little one, settle in this, relax in this, My tender embrace, and let Me hold you always, always, always in love.

"My God, my very own God."

Marie M. Constance

Yes, your very own. Come. I desire to hold you.
"Yes, Lord. Oh, to be so blessed!"
Oh, to be so loved! Come. Just be, and let Me flow through.

☙❧

We're getting a nice snow.

With it
Comes a stillness
That is blessed.

All things at night
Now seem stilled.

At peace.

Looking out my window
At the street,
The houses,
The trees,

All seems quiet and lulled.

My heart too
Rests now
In happy stillness
After the turmoil has ceased.

Oh God, in this expression
Of Your great peace,
In Your eternal quiet,
Let me find glimpses
Of You

And feel
Sweet perceptions
Of Your loving presence.

Help me grow
To be more prepared,
More aware,
More alive
In You.

I love the snow.
I love the beauty
You bring
To everything
In the quiet snow.

My Lord, it is You
I love.

Whenever I love
Anyone or anything,
It is always You.

My grace is like snow. When conditions are just right, it comes, falling gently, making all things beautiful.
"What conditions?"
Receptivity. Yes, My dear, and prayer increases receptivity. Listen carefully now to this I wish to tell you.
"Guide me."
I, your Lord, I, your life, I, your beloved, am the Lord of all, am the life of all, am the beloved of all. I seek to be known as such. I seek receptive hearts. When I find receptive hearts, I come to bestow My blessings. I come to love. I come to reveal Myself. I come to receive love. I come to become those who would receive Me. You, My child, have received Me. You

have loved Me. You have let Me love you, and you have let My love flow through. When you desire that another also receives Me and enjoys Me in all My fullness, this is truly My desire. I, God of all, desire to give Myself to all, yet I may give only to those who would receive. You help them want to receive.

This I want of you. Help them want Me, child. Help Me awaken the same desire in them so, in desiring each other, I shall be one with them, they in Me, I in them. I love you, My dear. How I love you. Know My love, My child. Know My love and thus know Me! In loving Me you receive Me. In receiving Me you love Me. On and on, there is no middle, only one loving, one love, forever and ever, My child. Now, always, forever, one love I am.

☙❧

> Oh, let my soul
> Be like a budding flower,
> My Lord,
> Opening up
> To the light of Your presence,
> Pouring forth
> Sweet fragrances
> Of inner devotions,
> Crying out
> In love of You!
>
> You are my adored
> Forever and ever,
> My Lord
> And my God!

Oneness is like sunlight, My dear.
"Sweet Jesus, I love Your light."
Be like this plant, My dear. Turn toward My light. Ever seek and live in My light! Feel and know this. It is Me. I am the love. I am the energy. I

am the words. I am the essence that flows through. Drink in My life, My dear, as the plants drink in the rain. Do not think you will be aware of My light's passage from you to another. Look at the plants. Can you see their reception of light? No, but you know it occurs. You know this, and you expect the plants to grow. So shall it be with those who receive My light as I channel it through you. You will not see it, but you must grow in faith that it will occur, and then expect growth.

You must trust in My infinite wisdom and believe I see all things and know the best course for each and every one of My children. Just let go of trying to see, and let Me be in you. If you remain in Me and listen to My voice, you and I shall bring much grace to those in need. I hear your every prayer. I know your every thought, and each and every person you point out to Me, I bless. Believe Me. When you pray for all, My dear, I bless all. Now, feel My light. I am going to show you the meaning of My words, but do not become preoccupied with thinking about this or about anything else. Occupy your thoughts with Me. Let all else come to you as easily as the dawn comes to light. It will come. Rejoice, My dear. Rejoice!

"Oh my Lord, how You inflate my being. I am rejoicing, my Lord. I am. Thank You! Forever and ever, thank You."

Come.

༺☙༻

My heart is melting
In the warmth
Of Your love,
Oh God
Of all!

I come to You,
Asking
As a child
Asks his father
Or mother,

Asking You
To reveal Yourself
To those I bring
To the altar
Of Your presence.

Bless them each and all
With Your most tender
Touch of love!

"Jesus, with all my heart I ask You to bless those dearest to me with Your all-pervading love."

It is done. You see, My child, because My love is all pervading, they are already so blessed. They are always so blessed. They must awaken into this understanding. When they do not know My love, they are living in delusion, but when they realize My love, all will be new for them, and they will begin to understand the true nature of their existence.

"Then my Lord, how should I pray for them? Tell me how to pray for them. I know You want me to pray, but what is the best prayer, one that is most pleasing to You, my beloved?"

This is how I want you to pray, My child. First, empty yourself. Center yourself. Seek Me first. Seek and live in My love. When you enter My heart of love, then ask for their awakening. Bring them to Me. Bring them into this love that I am. But it is best if you enter first and then ask for them to enter as well.

Chapter Eleven

To realize
I live
But by
Your breath alone.

Oh, intoxication divine!

Your breathing
Into me
Is like a kiss
So sweet,
So ever new.

Ever blissful,
It is ever You!

"My Lord, my Lord. I am calling You."
I love you, My child. Think about this. You know how you long for your loved ones just to let you hold them close to your heart? Remember how you used to want to hold your babies all day long, feeling their sweet little innocence melt into your being, how you would feel so united with them

that tears would fill your eyes, and sweet warmth would flow through your being just from holding them?

"Yes, my Lord, I remember, and what a sweet happy memory!"

All that sweetness was of Me, is of Me. I am this sweetness. I am this love. I am this longing. Now, I tell you this: I long for My little ones to let Me hold them close to My heart too. I long to hold you, My child, so whenever you call upon Me, let Me hold you, and find your true happiness in My embrace.

☙❧

Use my heart today, Lord,
Oh compassionate one,
As Your instrument of love.

Send Your love divine
Through my heart
To those You wish
To draw unto You.

As the light of the sun's rays
Is concentrated
Through the magnifying glass,
Inflaming the objects reflected upon,
So use my heart
To concentrate Your rays
Of all-pervading light and love,
To shine upon those
For whom You wish me to pray,
Today
And every day.

Oh Lord, help me
To be ever
Your willing instrument,

Ready and open
For You to love me
And those for whom Your spirit
May prompt me to pray.

Help me remember
To fulfill my daily duties
With the thought
I am doing everything
For You.

Doing for my children and husband
Is actually doing for You
Because You are in them,
They in You.

Teach me to develop
The right attitude,
Oh spirit of goodness and virtue.

I love You, my Lord!

"When You said, *Bring them to Me*, did You mean I may bring them to You in prayer, that out of love for them I may really bring them to You? I don't understand because it seems You would bring them to Yourself with or without me."

No, My child. I need your cooperation. They need your prayers. You increase their receptivity when you pray for them, and if you love them as you pray then it is easier for them to come to Me. It is love that performs the miracle of their transformation. I am the love, but you are My channel. Recall the image of the magnifying glass. It may help you understand. Your prayers, with love, may be like the magnifying glass. My light is all around, but, when it is concentrated through the lens of your heart and prayers, they may receive it more intensely, more completely.

Marie M. Constance

"Oh Lord of light and truth, I am Yours. Do with me as You will!"

☙

We breathe the same air.
We touch the same earth.

Do we have the same life
Within us?

Can we touch
The same source
Of this life,
The same cause
When we look within?

Can we feel and know
The same joy
That is released
When one of us finds
What we seek?

Can one give
To the other?

Can one open the door
For the other
If it is out of love?

Can one uplift the other
While being lifted
In joy?

Can this life within,
Flowing upward,

Living Reality

Find a channel
Through the eyes
Of one
And, gushing forth,
Then flow through the eyes
Of the other
And fill that one too?

I shall ask.
I shall knock.
I shall persist
Until in joy
I hear the eternal yes!

"My Lord, can I bring anyone on this path with me?"

Each has his own path. This one is yours, My child, but know I bless your dear ones as you walk this path with Me. They need not be on the path with you to receive My blessings.

"Can my prayers for them help them clear their own paths?"

Yes, child. Continue to pray for them. Continue to bring them to Me, and in this you are clearing the channel to them, the channel of My river of love. I have told you before, and I tell you again: You are My channel.

"Cleanse me, Lord, empty me that there will be no obstacles to the flood of Your love."

Overcome all by loving all. Love Me in them and them in Me. See Me. Know I am truly in all, though hidden in some more than others. I cannot force My love. Your prayers help them turn to Me, so I may wash them and bathe them in My love. Come now, and receive My blessing. Receive My love!

"Lord, I have written so much already today. Is there anything else You wish me to write?"

Only that I want you to be happy in My love. I want you to smile, My child, and My love will flow through you to others. Even when you are alone, smile. The energy will continue out into the world. You see, as I told you, My love will flow through in ways you never would imagine. Live in My love. Live ever and ever in Me!

Marie M. Constance

☙❧

Once again
I am drinking deeply
Of the sweet nectar,
Of love within.

Oh, the joy
That flows in this!

I must constantly
Call His name
Or pray
Without ceasing
Whenever I am between actions,
For such a flood
Is pushing through
My every pore!

In activity
I must subdue this
Enough to perform,
Yet in every pause
Such intoxicating joy
Comes over me.

I can only turn to Him
And cry,
"My God, my God, my God!
I love You, oh my God,
My Lord, my life,
My love, my all!"

In this blessed joy,
I remember
All who are dear to me.

I ask Him to bless
Each and all
With this love,
With this joy.

I was trying to tell you about My not forcing My love on them. Sometimes they become aware of My presence only when there is trouble or pain. Only then do they see My hand. But you, little one, have come to Me not only in pain but also in joy. This does please Me so.
"What else do You wish to tell me?"
Thank you for looking for Me in the full light, not just in the shade. Come and find out why My hand is always outstretched caressingly.
"I want to know. I want to see, but most of all I want to return my love for Yours, though it is so little."
You know how I feel about little.
"Jesus, You are so sweet. You are so good to me. I love You."
This I long to hear you say to Me as often as you wish. You come that much closer each time you say it.
"I long to please You. I am so happy in knowing it pleases You when I tell You I love You. There is nothing I'd rather say to You, except to vary the words so that, if possible, I may say this in the most tender ways."
My dear one, you may vary the expressions of your heart a thousand ways more than with words. So begin with the words, and then, to please Me even more, turn them into wordless adorations. These I will receive and, My child, I will return!
"Oh my beloved Lord God, prompt me in whatever way is most pleasing to You. How I long to know I am pleasing You. I love You, my Lord. I love You."
Come. Begin now.

Marie M. Constance

☙❧

Oh my Lord,
You have given me
This love for my dear ones.

Sometimes it is so intense,
So strong!

Oh, the sweet pain
Of love's abundance,
Of love's longing
To be received.

Deep, deep, deep within
Does Your river
Begin to flow
Now in my heart.

I feel its rushing waters
Gushing through,
Seeking another vessel,
Another vein
Therein
To be contained,
To fill and renew,
To continue on through.

Tell me
Where I may
Direct the current,
Oh master
Of the water's will!

Living Reality

Love them now, My dear. Love them beyond word, beyond thought, beyond sense. Into the purest essence of My love do you bring them when you love them in this way. This, My dear, is My desire. Melt into this that I am and bring them tenderly into this with you. Lead them in, My dear. Show them how desirable I am. How desirous I am of their entering the essence of this, My love. Bring them into this, My loving you!

"Oh Jesus, what a blessed, blessed task. How You inflate my being simply with this request. Now to do it! Oh, blessed, blessed loving. Oh, blessed, blessed being. Oh, blessed, blessed love divine, my only reality, my very own God."

Tell them with all the love in your heart, My dear, yet without words convey this to them. Oh, please convey that I am God, and I desire to love them each and all, that I am each one's very own God. Imagine if all knew they own Me in this, My desire to love. Imagine if they knew! Oh, what a world this could be, and My dear, they shall know. Yes! Rejoice, My precious little messenger. Rejoice, for they shall know because of you. They shall know because of your prayer and because of your writings, but most of all, My dear, they shall know because of your love for Me, for your dears, for all. You do love all, don't you?

"Yes, Lord, although I know it is You. It can only be You. Otherwise how could I love them all?"

Precisely, My dear. You see, love comes automatically as a result of your surrender to My loving you. You automatically love those I love because you enter My love, the universal love. Oh, My precious one, do you see how love is the cure for all that plagues My people? Yes! And as one enters My love, so do all enter. I am love. I am in all. All are in Me. I am one. All are one in Me. In reality this is always true, yet most know it not. It is My grace to grant increase in receptivity when one turns to Me, when one comes to Me, and when one enters My heart of love through prayer and devotion to My way, to Me. When one enters, the motion of My grace increases and flows to all. That is how one may help all. Do you see?

"Continue, please."

Your prayer, your devotion, and your entering cause this increase in the flow of My grace. It is out of your free will, your choice, that you enter. That is your part, My dear. The rest is My grace. So do this as often as you may. Do this for Me, for yourself, for all.

"Oh my God, how wonderful, how unbelievable, yet how true. Teach me more, my Lord. Teach me more!"

I shall teach you much, much more when you do as I ask. Enter now, My dear, and bring all in.

"Yes, my loving Lord. Yes!"

CB EO

Oh, how sweet this time
Alone with my Lord.

How wonderful!

My heart cries out,
"Oh joy, oh wonder, oh love!"

Continuous
Flowing,
Surging,
These sweet perceptions
Of one so near,
One so dear.

I am swimming in a sea of bliss,
Diving deep
In search of more treasure
Though I have more than enough
To last forever.

Still He bids me
Dive deep,

Living Reality

Deeper still,
To be held
Still
So as not to ripple
The clear, blue, reflective waters.

Oh, refreshing waters!

Oh, sweet the stillness.
Oh, tender the embrace.

I am held as I swim,
As I dive,
As I cease motion.

I am held continuously
In my Lord's embrace.

And as I whisper my gratitude
I whisper too of my dears,
Asking,
Hoping
They too might be held
While they swim,
While they dive,
While they work,
While they rest,
While they pray,
While they are still.

Held continuously in Him!

I require this of you, Marie. Yes, require. In order that you may continue on this journey, I desire that you stop here and receive refreshment and nourishment. Drink deeply of My living water, and come! Enjoy a swim with Me. Dive deep in My waters of love, Marie dear. Oh, how I look forward with delight to those days you stop along the way to be refreshed and renewed in My hospitality before you continue on your journey. Come, enjoy this meal, this drink, this swim with and in Me, within Me.

"My precious, precious God."

My precious, precious one, come. Enjoy! This is a requirement, yes, but it requires your yes as well.

"Then I say yes. Yes shall be my echoed response, my most dear hospitable one."

Come. I have awaited this day. Oh, My dear, how I delight in your happy company.

"And how I delight in Yours."

Then let us, full of delight, be in each other's company this entire day. Come, My dear, and stay.

"My Lord?"

Yes, My dear?

"Will You care for my companions too?"

Of course, My dear. I shall feed and nourish, refresh and renew all whom you bring here with you. I welcome and delight in all who come here, and there is plenty for all, for I am the ever-renewable source of all nourishment and refreshment. Bring them all here with you, My dear. Bring your dears. Bring all! For all are in need of stopping along the way to be refreshed and renewed in My company, in My hospitality, in My love, in Me. So come. Bring them all. Bring them all here with you so they might receive in Me as you receive in Me and be thus filled to overflowing with all that flows from My ever-abundant, all-fulfilling, ever-flowing, never-ending love divine.

"My precious, precious, precious God!"

My little one, My delightful one, My dear. Stay a little longer, child. Please, stay a little longer. Come into Me. Let Me love you.

ॐ

Oh my Lord,
I love!
I love to the point of tears.

It is as if I turn
Inside out
With the intensity
Of love's outpouring
From within.

I concentrate this love
On individuals
For whom I am prompted
To pray
Then I concentrate
Just on the love.

Oh, pure love!

Then all is You,
My Lord.
All is You.

Take me, my Lord.
Hold me
In the all-ness of You!

"My Lord, I forget to pray for so many when I become so absorbed in Your love. Tell me which You prefer in my prayer."

I prefer that you come to Me, enter, and receive. Then and most of all do I bless you and those in your heart. For when you enter, you bring them all to Me in your heart, both those you remember and those you forget, for your heart holds them all. That is why I always ask you to come, enter, and receive. This is the higher prayer, My dear. Will you do as I ask?

"Oh my Lord, take my hand and lead me. I love You!"

ೋ ೋ

Marie M. Constance

Love grows
Nourished by itself,
Continuing on its own,
Never diminishing,
Never ending,
Always onward,
Increasing,
Spreading,
Filling.

Sweet, endless love!

Today my prayer
Is that He would bless me
So I not only love
My dear ones
In feeling,
And in tenderness,
But in action as well.

May His love find its way
Through my heart,
Into my hands and feet,
Through my eyes and my voice,
My life!

I pray also for my loved ones.

May He thus bless them as well,
First in the most tender,
Endearing flow of sweet love
In their hearts,
And then
May it flow onward,
Increasing, spreading, filling.

Oh, this sweet, endless love.
What a wonderful God!

"My Lord, I bring them to You now."

Yes My child. Keep bringing them to Me. Keep loving them as you bring them. Fill your heart with My love, and then surround them with this love whenever you think of them. It is not necessary for you to empty and enter each time you wish to bring them. Just remember to keep My love alive in your heart, and place them ever so gently in this love, as if you were placing your dear little babies in their cradles. What better cradle than My love?

The highest service you can do for mankind, Marie, is to hold all in this that I am, and if you hold all daily in this then you serve all daily, and if I am in all then you serve Me in this way, in the highest way. You see, My dear, I have heard your thoughts of your desire to give, of your doubts that you do give and your doubts that you are giving. Bring them here, My dear. In this bringing you are giving more than you could ever give in any other way. Believe this, My dear. This is My truth! You give most in your prayer, more than you ever could in those ways you have imagined. So, My dear, do this. Do this for them and for Me.

"Yes, my Lord. I love you."

Yes, My dear, and I love you. Know this. Always know that I love you.

"Jesus?"

Yes?

"I am at a loss for words, but my pen is in my hand. What would You have me write?"

This, My child, Marie. This: I love you dearly. I love all My children dearly. I long for you to come to Me and receive My love. I long for all My children to come to Me and receive My love. They forget this. They forget that My main message is that I love them. I am love.

"What do You want me to do?"

Keep writing. Keep praying. Keep loving. Keep listening. Keep your heart open to Me, and My love will flow through to them.

Lesson Five: Manifest

I wish for you to make known My love.
I wish for you to make known My joy.

Chapter Twelve

How my Lord feeds me while I am performing the simplest tasks! How He is answering my prayer that He show me how beautiful simplicity is and how extraordinary the ordinary. How my heart soars as I feel the next step approaching.

At first when I contemplate the word *manifest*, it scares me, but if manifesting is part of His will, what is there to fear other than unbearable joy? Only He can give me the grace to enter the next step, so in the meantime all I am to do is remain, receive, be open, and be. Oh, how I feel it coming, this wondrous message of love, of Him made manifest in words, from His word, from and in His love, from and in Him for all. I feel as if He now wants to tell all how He feels about them, how He loves them, how He longs for them, how He desires their fulfillment, how He yearns for their love in return, and how He yearns for their openness to His all-fulfilling love! He longs to reveal all this and more. Oh, blessed, blessed love divine. I melt; I fly; I cry; I love in this.

When I feel His intense, intoxicating, yet intimate and tender love, He often gives some practical guidance to go along with it. I have great difficulty accomplishing anything when His touch melts me! He helps me attend to matters at hand whenever I am drunk on such overwhelming love. For example, one day He led me into understanding more about doing little things for Him while in His Love. He told me He wanted me to give Him glory in every little thing I do. The next day He went on further to explain that by seeing Him in all things, all people, and all events, and by staying in Him in all I do, He may live in and through me, and we may always be one and share every experience.

He told me: *Every little detail of your life, of your day, can actually be in essence a working out of salvation. See the hidden nature of all things as a microcosm of all.* He said I should begin to see all things anew, and He would give me eyes to see and ears to hear, adding, *Just call My name, and be aware that you are becoming today.*

On that particular day, I felt a new awareness, though it was not constant. Rather I was in and out of awareness of another dimension. I felt the intensity in the flow of energy in my body coming and going too as I went about my housework that day. Even when I ate, I was aware of the systems in my body at work. When I washed dishes, I felt the life in the energy that moved my arms and hands, and I felt the same in my feet and legs when I walked. It was not a constant awareness but more like a tuning in and out.

Sometimes, while I am washing dishes, folding laundry, or performing some other housework, He enters into the activity, causing me to long for the action to be prolonged, so close does He become in the action. I recall a day when something was revealed to me on a level of understanding that seemed to connect the tangible with the intangible. I was helping my husband take off his work boots, and then his socks, and as I touched his bare feet I was struck by an image of the feet of Jesus. I felt connected in that little act of love with the very person of my God, feeling that my husband's feet could very well be His feet. Then I realized that anything I did for my husband could be for Him, and not just in symbol or offering but really for the person, Jesus, in the person of my husband or any other person for whom I might perform an act of love.

I have had other similarly distinct experiences wherein I have felt a mysterious link between the corporeal and ethereal. Once, while I was vacuuming the floor, I suddenly felt as if His hands were in mine, and His arms were around me, helping me in that seemingly insignificant task. I realized nothing I do in Him, with Him, or for Him is ever insignificant. All is sacred when done in awareness of Him.

How extraordinary that some of the most striking revelations come in the simplest tasks! Once, while I was washing dishes, I felt His certain presence behind me quite clearly, as if He were right there in back of me while I stood at the sink. Suddenly I felt as if He stepped into me from behind, as if His person, His body, stepped into my person, my body, and then I felt as if my hands had become His hands, and He moved them while performing the task of washing the dishes. I did not simply visualize that transformation, as I did not initiate it in thought but felt it first then thought about it afterward.

In another encounter I felt the purest, sweetest, most unconditional love flowing through my mind and heart as He explained to me that if I were to wash dishes while in full awareness of His presence in and with me, I could offer that task as another "act of love" for all people. While considering the idea of consecrating all my thoughts, words, and deeds through acts of love and pondering the meaning of the microcosm, I suddenly became aware of many, many people in need. He then helped me see that by washing dishes, I could be cleansing those in need of Him so they could receive nourishment from Him.

Suddenly that analogy was extremely clear to me as I thought about the function of cleaning the utensils. Food would be received in a pure state only if served with clean utensils; otherwise food could spoil, taste poor, or not be received properly. He showed me as I wiped each utensil clean that each person could receive more purely and more completely by that very process of cleansing (symbolic yet real) if it were performed prayerfully in and with Him. Wiping each utensil clean was actually a kind of bringing-in prayer. I felt that prayer in my heart, and I felt His using my action for them.

As His revelations have almost always come with tears, of course in that experience I cried as I loved Him with each movement of my arms and hands, and I loved those in need too though I did not know who they were. As a matter of fact, when I first started perceiving what was going on, I started trying to identify each utensil with a particular individual or group. Immediately I knew He did not want me to impose such limits; rather He wanted me to let go of "who" and just do it!

To balance the tears, I also perceived in that parallel a bit of humor as I sensed that adored twinkle in His eye. By the time I had finished washing the dishes, I was quite intoxicated by the unique experience. I remember thinking that when I was not aware of Him in that task, it always seemed there was no end to the number of utensils. However, after performing the washing of each fork, each spoon, and each knife as if each were so vital in the way He was receiving my act of love, I was actually disappointed when the task was finished. He told me He would multiply those acts of love for all.

Working in the garden has also provided opportunities for me to offer acts of love. One morning, when the energy I felt from Him was very intense, He invited me to work in the garden with Him in a way that I might use some of that energy together with Him, as part of the microcosm. As I hoed and pulled weeds, He instructed me again with the use of allegory. After I thought, *This weed is kind of pretty, so I think I'll leave it*, he instructed me not to be fooled by the pretty ones. He told me to pull them all out by the roots and to do a thorough job and not leave any roots behind. In some ways such allusions applied to me, but mostly I felt as if I were helping Him in the job of weeding on a larger scale.

Wiregrass was also in the lesson when He showed me how it cleverly intertwined itself with the plants and how it was hard to see and even harder to pull out by the roots because it would pull up the roots of the other plants too. He asked me to remove those weeds carefully, taking great care not to pull out the other plants and not to leave any roots of the wiregrass behind, and to do a good job.

The following morning I weeded in a different garden, where wiregrass was trying to spread. He pointed out how it was easier to remove here because I had used mulch. The wiregrass was sending out shoots all over the place, but they were only in the mulch and were easy to dig up because the mulch was loose, making it easy to work things out. He explained how the flowers in that garden could flourish because of the mulch, and the weeds could flourish, but the work of the gardener would be easier because of the mulch. He made an analogy between the mulch and people. He showed me other things too about the gardening process and how I could really help Him. I understood that my prayer could be much like the mulch and the hoe as I recalled His words: *prayer increases receptivity.*

Prayers for others are often accompanied by a burning sensation in my heart. It is a desirable fire that seems to spread as I attend to it. I become intoxicated by the blissfulness, and I wish to give of myself to my God and to my loved ones. A question always arises: how? The answer seems to vary according to the time and place in which I ask. If I'm active at the moment, the answer usually applies to the task at hand: *Make it better,* or *Bring Me into your task.* If I'm in prayer, the answer is, *Intensify,* or *Surrender,* or *Go deeper.* Though different, the answers are truly one and the same: *Intensify your attention to Me* whether in action or in the stillness of prayer. All should be prayer. All can be prayer. I may always have Him near and love Him in all I do. That is how—by being attentive to Him in all I do. In this I love Him, and I love my dear ones as well.

Chapter Thirteen

Instead of expressing Your love
In ink
Today, my Lord, help me
Be open
So Your precious love current
Will flow through my hands,
Not through my pen
But through my work
Here at home.

Often I have left my work
To write to You,
For You,
For those I love.

Today, help me
Turn from writing
Back to work,
Creatively expressing
Your love
In humble ways.

Stay ever and ever with me,
My dearest, my sweetest,
My ever-loving Lord!

Proceed with the lessons I have given you, and then, My dear...
"What, my Lord?"
Then I shall reveal the next step in the next lesson.
"Oh my Lord, now? I hear a word surfacing."
What is it, My dear?
"Manifest."
Yes, that is the next step and the next lesson, but do not begin trying to manifest yet, My dear. There is still preparation in the first four lessons. Think Me always. Accept humbly all that comes your way, and in this you will learn to trust more. Remain in Me. Receive all My gifts and blessings, and be open so all shall flow through. Then, My dear, when I tell you, you shall begin to manifest.

Now I wish to tell you what I want of you besides your coming to Me, besides your letting Me love you. I wish for you to make known My love. I wish for you to make known My joy. Here is how you are to proceed: Continue to write daily. Continue to meditate on My love daily. Continue to pray for all daily. Continue to talk to Me daily. Soon, My child, we shall find the way that is best for you to make known My revelation of love. You know it. You feel it. You enjoy it. Now become it. Become My love. Become Me!

"How can this be? Show me what You mean. You can do all things. Reveal to me the meaning of Your words."

I said I am preparing you. You want to know what for? For becoming a living embodiment of love. You are becoming love, My dearest. Love!

"I still do not grasp this, Lord. It is so incredible."

You do not need to grasp it. All you need to do is say yes. I will do the rest.

"Then yes. A thousand times yes. Forever and ever yes! Is that all?"
That is all.

☙❧

Marie M. Constance

My Lord,
Within my heart
I find such fires of love!

Glowing, blazing flames
Burning sweetly,
Shining brightly
For my dearest ones.

Bless them too my God,
Enkindling within
The sweetest fires
Of burning love for You.

I offer these flames, oh Lord,
Back to You,
My innermost core.

Let these
Fires within
Always burn for You,
And then,
If it is Your will
Let them burn for Your friends
And lovers too.

Take me, oh blessed one,
And love through me,
Lest the pain of love's abundance
Consuming me
Will be too much to bear.

Prepare me, Lord.
Purify me, oh my beloved,
Ever in the fires of love!

Do you see how all flows so sweetly when you simply let go and let Me?

"Yes I do. Sometimes I wonder how long this can continue. Then I realize even to think in such a way is limiting, so I just let go, and then I feel the increase again."

Yes. You are a good pupil, My dear. Keep on listening and learning.

"Oh, my most wondrous teacher, how I love You!"

Yes, you do, don't you? Come. Carry this sweetness wherever you go, and let it flow to whomever you greet.

"Yes, Lord. Lord?"

Yes, My dear?

"Hold my dear ones as You hold me."

I am holding them. You see, I felt and knew your prayer even before you asked. You are in Me, My dear, and I automatically hold them as I hold you because you hold them in your heart.

"Sometimes, though, isn't there increase for them as well?"

Oh, yes! Yes, there is increase for all in this, your unity with Me, your oneness in Me. Keep on, My dear. Remain in Me. Receive and be open.

"Lord?"

Yes, I know your next question, My dear. You want to know if the next lesson has begun. Yes, My dear, it has, and I repeat, it continues out of all previous lessons. Each one continues and grows into the next. Yes, My dear, now we manifest.

"You said 'we.'"

Yes, always this applies. My grace makes all this possible—My grace and your efforts. Together we do these works. I teach. You listen and learn. You let go and let Me. Especially now, My dear, in this next lesson, "Manifest." You must grow into this and continue to let Me teach you how to remain in Me, how to receive and be open, and then I manifest through you. Do you see?

"I think so."

Yes, you have partial vision now, but I'm increasing that as well. The more you let go, the more you let Me, the more I may increase My blessings upon, within, and through you.

"Hold me, Lord!"

I am. Come, let's be off.

"Yes, Lord."
My dear?
"Yes, Lord?"
Do not try to understand. Just let Me show you. Let it all unfold.
"With sweetest, sweetest pleasure. How gracious You are!"
In return you may be gracious too, My dear. Be a gracious receiver, please.

☙❧

>Oh my God,
>I am in love
>With You!
>
>My heart of hearts,
>Absorbed
>In such sweetness,
>Yet such pain
>Cries for completeness.
>
>How I long
>To be completed in You!
>
>My only desire
>Now, my God,
>Is to be
>Ever and ever
>One
>With You!

It is My desire that you become completely united with Me, My dear. Know this is My desire.
"My Lord, I melt. I know not what to say or do. I simply melt in Your presence. Hold me. Forever hold me."

Living Reality

Listen to Me. Realize I am this for you. Love Me in this. Receive Me in this. Come. All you do, all you say, all you are shall flow out of this unity with Me. Come, My dear. Let Me complete that which I have begun.

⊰ ⊱

"My Lord and my God!"

These words,
Repeated
Over and over,
Have become part of my being.

They have carried me
Into a more continuous awareness
Of Your presence,
My Lord and my God.

It is within my heart,
Oh my Jesus,
That I shout with joy
And proclaim Your glory.

Let my heart, oh my dearest,
Be ever aware of You,
So you might use me
To love Your dear ones,
And let Your light radiate
From this center of my being,
This place where I find You!

Go in My peace. Stay in My love, and let My love flow through in your actions and your prayers. Relax, My child, and enjoy! I will guide you always, and if you have questions, then ask. Ask Me. Live in Me, and find all answers in Me.

"Thank You, my Lord, for Your peace, for Your love."
Come now, let us enjoy each other's company.
"Oh, blessed, blessed lover of my heart and soul!"
Speak tenderly to Me. Speak tenderly in the silences of your heart.
"I will, Lord."
And I will do the same.
"Lead me in the song."
I will be the harmony.

☙❧

Jesus, oh my Jesus!

How my heart yearns
For You.
How my whole being
Cries out
For love of You,
For want
Of Your love,
For me.

Take me,
My Jesus.
Take me
Into Your heart
And make me one
Forever and ever
With You!

Now, my Lord,
You must show me the way—
The way to stay with You,
The way to be attentive to You,
The way to love You

Living Reality

All throughout my day
No matter where I am
Or what I'm doing.

Keep me ever and ever
Attuned to You!

Oh, how I want to love You
With all my heart and soul.
With all that I am,
forever loving You.

I'm looking for You now,
My sweet one.
Don't hide Your face from me.

I will find You within,
In the center of my being,
Waiting to receive me
As I learn to give myself to You
In stillness.

I do love You, my Lord.

Teach me how to love You
More and more,
Forever and ever.
Amen!

"What would You have me write, my Lord?"
That I want you ever at My side. I want you to stay ever with Me and in Me. I want you, Marie, to be ever Mine.
"Am I not Yours already?"
Not completely.
"How may I become completely Yours?"

Stay ever in Me. Always listen. Listen for My voice. Listen for My instructions, and most of all listen for My love.

"Listen for Your love? Explain, please, my Lord."

My love is within. My love is sweet. My love is deep. Listen as you go deep within in search of My sweetness. There you will receive My love and My instructions with your innermost being. There you will truly hear. There you will truly see. There you will truly know.

"Oh my Lord, my life, take me there!"

Come in. Come in, My beloved, and hear My voice. Come in, and see My face. Come in, and know Me.

"My Jesus, thank You!"

Let Me thank you with My love. Oh, My child, come in and let Me love you.

"Oh my Lord, I am Yours."

And I, My child, am yours.

"Show me how truly to come in."

Take My hand. Let go of all else. Listen. Lift your eyes. Breathe. Breathe My name. Be still. Feel My love. Cease all thought except for and of Me, and come!

☙❧

My Jesus,

When I look at the blue sky,
I think of You.

Are Your eyes so blue?

When I feel the breeze,
I breathe in Your sweetness of breath.

Are Your lungs yet fully grown lilies
Floating on the waters?

Living Reality

When the soft light of the setting sun
Seeps in through my eyes,
I feel You
Warming my heart.

Are Your hands
But purely burning flames?

Oh, my beloved!

Let me see not the sky
But Your eyes.
Let me breathe not air
But Your breath.
Let me feel not sunlight
But Your hands upon my heart.

Oh my Jesus,

Let me know not part
But all of You!
Then I may love not a portion
But the whole You.

You want my love?
Then reveal Yourself to me!

My Lord,
What is this pull
At my heart?
What is this
That calls me to love?

Is it You?
Is it Your touch?

> Tell me the truth,
> My Lord,
> And reveal Yourself
> To me!

"Lord, You are too good to be true."

But I am true. I am always true—to My word, to My beloved children. Be true to Me, My child, and you will always be true to others. You will do My will, and you will know My happiness. So, My dear little one, Marie, follow My example and always be true, and you will also find yourself in goodness. Someone may even say of you, "You are too good to be true."

"I don't want anyone to say that. Let them see only You and say that about You."

My child, fear not. You need not be concerned with what they may say. Just live in Me, and all will be well. If you must, hide yourself in Me.

"Show me how."

Fear not. I am your guide. Take My hand, My sweet one, and walk with Me. Always walk with Me.

"My Lord, I love You. Oh, how I love You!"

Come. Let us make this our day. Let us spend every moment together in joy, enjoying each other's company.

"I always enjoy Your company, but I forget that You enjoy my company. I forget this."

Never forget I love and cherish you and long for you always to remain at My side. Talk to Me, child. Talk to Me about anything you like. I await your calling upon Me. I love to hear you use My name. Come and talk to Me.

"Not only will I use Your name, but I will hold Your name in my heart, and then everything will whisper Your name to me. I hear it in the breeze. I hear it in the kids' singing. I hear it in footsteps. I hear it in my heartbeat. I hear it in the silences. I hear and I feel Your name everywhere!"

Keep hearing, keep listening, and you shall be full of the sound of My love. Listen and hear. Know My love. Know Me!

Living Reality

☙❧

Vivid is the image of You,
My beloved, my Lord,
Holding me in Your hands.

Now as clear
Yet more sweet
Is this perception of You,
My beloved, my Lord,
Holding me in Your heart.

As I take up
My daily tasks,
I feel You are with me,
You are in me,
Lifting my hands,
Moving my feet.

The clearer You become,
The more graceful become
My motions,
The more motionless my pauses,
Until I feel as if in a ballet,
Each movement flowing gracefully
From the pause,
Each breath from breathlessness,
Each pulse from a heart held still
By Your touch
Until I enter more deeply
Into each rest
Between motions,
Between breaths,
Between heartbeats.

As I become more aware of You
In and out,
Within and without,
All becomes one.

There is in truth
Only You.

I realize
I am in You
In motion,
In stillness,
In love.

Always in You,
Always in love.

Oh, blessed, blessed oneness!

"My sweet one, my Lord, my adored one, I love You."
And I, My delightful one, love you. You are My delight when you let Me love you so. Come, My little one. Come. Delight Me!
"Lead me, Lord."
Take My hand.
"Show me how truly to take Your hand."
I've been waiting for you to ask this question.
"You have?"
Yes. Now that you have asked, I will tell you how. First, breathe My name. Lift your eyes. Feel My love encircling your heart.
"Yes, my Lord?"
Do this first, and then I will explain more.
"Help me to write Your explanations."
Proceed. When you feel My love encircling your heart, know it is My hand. And when you feel My love penetrating your heart, know that is

Living Reality

also My hand no longer hovering over but touching. And when you feel the sweetness permeating, know it also is My hand not merely touching but holding. And when you feel even more sweetness of love in the very center of your being, know it is also My hand not merely holding but caressing. In this, My child, you truly take My hand.

There is yet another way. When you lift your eyes and hold them thus and continue in this way as You breathe My name, you are looking for My hand and may then take it as your gaze becomes fixed, with your heart also fixed on My love. In this you truly take My hand.

There is yet another way. When you pray for another and let My love go out, encircling the prayed for; when you hold the image of another before Me, all the while sending love, peace, and joy; when you pray thus, My child, you truly take My hand.

So do you see why I say your hand is already in Mine? You are already doing what I have described for you. Yet you become more aware of My hand as you increase your efforts, as you increase your will to pray, as you increase your surrender to Me in all you do. As you let Me in, I bring you in more deeply. You shall thus grow in ever-increasing awareness of My hand ever holding you and those for whom you pray. Keep on, My child. I repeat: this is only the beginning!

∞

Beneath an anxiety
I've managed to find
A sweetness present
And a love burning.

For this entire time,
My heart and mind
Have kept repeating
Over and over and over,
"Jesus, Jesus, Jesus."

Can it be
This calling on Him
Over and over
Has put me in touch
With that inner sanctuary
I've been seeking?

Oh my Jesus, stay with me!

I know you are constantly thanking Me for all I am doing for you, with you, and in you, My dear. I receive all your gratitude. I receive all your thoughts, all your works, all your prayers, all your love. Just as you are receiving Me, My dear, I am receiving you, and you are becoming what I will you to become. Do you know this?

"Yes, Lord. Sometimes I am more aware than at other times. Sometimes I feel I have been unaware for a while, and then suddenly I return to awareness and wonder where I have been. Then I turn to You and say Your name, and it's as if I were never away."

You are never away from Me, My dear. I have told you many times, you are bound in love to Me. Do you believe this?

"Oh, yes, Lord, I do, and such peace comes in this believing. I want to say 'in this knowing,' but do I know?"

You are growing in knowledge as you are becoming. It is a process of awakening, an unfolding, a becoming, My dear. Trust in this process I have chosen for you. Trust in Me. Trust in your soul.

"Yes, Lord I'm trying."

Turn to Me! Let Me do it all. All you need is to try thinking always of Me, talking to Me, and loving Me in all you do. Be aware of Me! Call My name if you feel unaware.

"It is so simple, so sweet."

Be. Give by being.

"Is there anything You wish to say to me now, my Lord?"

Yes, My dear. When you see someone in pain, remember My pain. See Me in this, and when you empathize I receive your empathy. When you feel joy, remember My joy. See Me in this, and realize it is Me. See Me in all things, in all people, in all events. See Me and experience Me. Let Me live in and through you. Oh, My dear, that we should always be one, sharing all, doing all, experiencing all together! You and I, My dear, for your sake, for My sake, for the good of all. Every little detail of your life, of your day, can actually be in essence a working out of salvation. See the hidden nature of all things as a microcosm of all. Do you understand?

"Do I, Lord?"

Partly, but as I said, I shall reveal all to you. All I ask of you is that you stay in Me. You shall begin to see all things anew today. Yes, today you shall have eyes to see, My dear, and ears to hear. Just call My name, and be aware that today you are becoming.

"Yes, Lord. Receive my heart, mind, body, and soul today, now, so You will bless me with the ability to see and hear. I give myself to You now, Lord. Receive me!"

Receive Me, My dear. Receive Me.

☙❧

Intoxicated with You,
Oh Lord,
I know not
What to do.

Bubbling over and over
With the joy
Of Your nearness,
Your heartbeat,
Your love,
I cannot perform
Unless it is for You,
With You, and through You.

Lift my hands,
Move my feet,
Perform Your work
Through me,
My beloved,
My dearest,
My one!

Write that which I made known to you yesterday.
"About little things?"
Yes.
"You told me to give You glory in every little thing I do."
Do you recall what else I said?
"I'm trying to remember. Help me."
Did I not tell you how I long for your happiness? And I said I hate to see you suffer in any way.
"Yes, Lord, I remember now. I was thanking You after receiving reassurance when you lifted the doubt from me. You also said You hate for anyone to suffer, and You love all and long for all to know Your love."
Yes, I do. Now, My dear, how about some of this glory you've promised Me in all the little things you do?
"Jesus?"
Yes, My dear?
"Jesus, Your hands are so gentle."
Let this, My gentleness, flow through, My dear.
"I am Yours, my Lord. Use me as You will."
Then proceed. Proceed in My gentleness.
"Yes, Lord."
My dear, you caress My heart each time you perform an act of love, and do you know what an act of love is?
"Yes, Lord, I do."
Tell Me.

"An act of love is any action performed for You, with You in mind, in you, and in your love. Anything done in awareness of this can be an act of love. Is this right, Lord?"

Yes, My dear little one. Do you know that playing can also be an act of love?

"Yes, Lord. Anything, anything!"

Will you play with Me?

"How, my dearest?"

I shall teach you how to play.

"Do I need teaching?"

Yes. In some ways you have forgotten how to play, but you will remember, and you will learn new ways to play with Me.

"Teach me now."

Come. First we must work, but your work can be playful too, you know.

"Show me."

OK. Take My hand.

"Always and forever: Yes! Yes! Yes!"

Good. Let's be off. After you.

"My Lord, already You make me laugh."

Then you please Me. I like to hear you laugh, and I want you to smile as much as possible. Remember, your smile pleases Me so.

Chapter Fourteen

Crisp and clear the air,
Clearly reflective the waters,
Sweet the memory
Of being
Here
In this same spot
Along the river
Just a few months ago.

As I gaze out
Across the river,
I feel a difference
In the surrounding air.

It is fresh yet chilly,
And the fallen leaves
Contribute in their abundance
To the earthy aroma
I breathe.

The trees are different

Living Reality

Across the river,
Their autumn leaves warming
Both my mind and my heart
As they reflect the sun's gift
On branches,
On trunks,
On the flowing waters.

Oh, sweet light of the late
Afternoon sun!

Over my right shoulder,
I feel its presence.
In front I see its glory.

Soon no light will reflect
Off these beautiful trees
As darkness settles in

Yet oh, the remaining light
Still to reflect upon the waters
Through the night,
That sweet, sweet light of the moon,
Whose reflection already appears
Not ten yards in front of me
On the still, brown waters.

A few birds
Announce their presence
Here and there
In treetops nearby.
To whom are they speaking?
What news have they for passers-by?

With all my senses I rejoice

Marie M. Constance

In this autumn fare.
Yes! I can even taste the sweetness
Of dear, beloved nature
In the air.

And with another sense
More deep,
More subtly aware,
Do I perceive
Even sweeter glories
Before which all the rest
Merely bow in awe.

These, one may suspect,
Are revealed
Not in sight or sound,
Or touch or smell
Or even taste
But deeper and beyond.

They are reflections,
Perceptions,
Revelations
Of a greater light
To which all these beauties
Point,
From which all these beauties
Come.

A wondrous light,
A blessed light,
A joyous light
To my other sense is revealed
As I dive in and receive
His blessed love within.

Free yourself of all preconceived ideas. You limit Me. I want to reveal Myself as I am. Go beyond thought and sense. Come and see Me as I am. Be free. Let go.

"Show me how, Lord."

You know how, but, My dear one, take My hand. I will lead you. You must learn to release the importance you place on form and dive deeper into the essence. That is where I am. The form holds the essence, yet you must be able to perceive the essence. You, My child, are able, but I shall increase this ability as you let go. Go beyond thought and sense, My child. Then and there shall I be. Come. Come and see.

"Let me have Your hand."

It is beckoning. I am beckoning. I am waiting. Come, My dear. I await you.

"I love You, my Lord. Oh, how I love You!"

Come. Let Me show you how I love you.

☙❧

Oh, bittersweet pain,
You come to teach
Life's lessons.

You come to thrust us
Into the protecting
Embrace
Of life's truth:

I am beloved.
We are beloved.

Thrust into the arms
Of the beloved,
I am consoled.
I am soothed.
I am freed

From bitterness
And pain,
And drenched
In thy sweetness,

Ever convinced
I am
Beloved.

"My Lord, what now?"
Write.
"What would You have me write?"
Write this: I love you. I love all My children. I want My children to live not in fear but in peace. I want them to come to Me whenever they are having difficulty or pain. I want them to come to Me for comfort, for solace, for peace, for love. I want them to know Me as the comforter supreme, the eternal beloved.

Then they should not fear death but look forward to the day they are freed from the burdens and troubles of this world, freed to fly with Me as a bird who longs to be free of its cage. Suddenly the door is open. The outside of the cage is mostly an unknown, unfamiliar place, but the bird is meant to fly. The bird has wings. I gave the bird its wings. Until the bird flies, it does not know the reason for its wings. It can only speculate, imagine, dream.

Death, My child, is My servant. Death opens the door of the cage. I am both in the cage with the bird and outside the cage waiting, anticipating the bird's freedom and discovery of its wings, of the joy of flying, of the beauty of existence outside the cage, of joy and peace, of wonderful light, of wondrous bliss, of love ever new and unending, and of blessed oneness. I wait for all My children to discover and know this, each and every one!

○ॐ○

Oh, the pain
So many feel
When they know not
Your comfort, Lord!

Oh, the loneliness
When they know not
Your love!

Jesus, my Jesus,
What can I do?

What can I do?

"My Lord, when others are in pain, can I bring You to them? You ask me to bring them to You, but can I bring Your love to comfort them and give them solace?"

Yes, child, yes! And believe Me, you already have done this. Recall the comfort your father gave you as a child when you were sick. Do you remember how you felt the pain lift when he held you? So shall others' pain be lifted as you hold them. Touch those in pain. Touch them and pray. I will be there with you in your touch, child. I will touch them and lift their pain. Comfort them, hold them, love them, and I will flow through, as you asked. Remember, I hear and answer your every prayer, My dear little one.

☙❧

Father, You have given me
Four wonderful children
And a husband
Who is caring and loving,
Conscientious and hardworking.

For them
I am eternally grateful.

Bless them
In Your love and joy.

I am sorry for those times

I have not been grateful
To You, oh God,
For all Your wonderful gifts.

Bless me
So I remember You
Always
And keep a thankful heart
Ever alive with love for You!

Because of the tenderness your mother and father showed you when you were a child, you are able to come to Me and believe in My tenderness. Therefore you too must love tenderly so others may believe in My tenderness. Be sincere in your giving, in your loving. Be kind and compassionate. Be to them what I am to you. Then they shall begin to know how I love them. You are My channel. Love them, and I shall be the love!

"My Lord, You know how I am. I want to be still, just to melt in You, but I need to be present to those around me. Help me do this and not to remain stationary but to move, with You toward them."

My heart is moving through yours to them, My child. Think of Me. Think of Me holding those for whom you pray. Feel My love. Feel My love for them. Know My love! Then, My dear, you hold them too. Hold them in this love. No need to send it. I am here. You bring them to Me. You bring them into this love. It is the higher prayer. You already know My love for you and for your dear ones. Realize this love is for all. Bring all into this love that I am. Do you understand?

"Yes, Lord. I do. Already today I realized this higher prayer. I already know this love in part. I felt I should pour this very love into them. Now You show me I may put them in it. Is there a difference between pouring this love into them and putting them in it?"

Ah yes, My dear. There is a difference. Pouring is high. Bringing is higher. Entering is highest.

"This is so, so sacred. Do You wish for me to continue writing?"

Oh, yes, My dear, continue.

"What else do You wish for me to write?"
This: I love you. I am your God. I am your one beloved for all time. I am this for all. I love all. I am God of all. Know Me. Know My love. Know My peace. Know My truth. Come to Me, My dear little one, and let Me hold you. Let Me love you. Oh, how I long to love and to be received as joy, as sweetness, as love divine! Yet so many turn away from Me. You are My own little one. You listen to My words. You listen to My love. I long to give you all I have in store for you. Continue as I have instructed, and you shall receive. Oh, you shall receive! My dear, just come to Me. Simply come to Me without care. Place your cares before Me. Give them to Me. Let go and enter My love. Enter My heart. Enter My embrace. Enter Me!

"These are my cares, Lord. These."
I know, My dear. I know.

⌘

Oh, how glorious
The sun's rays are
When beaming
Through clouds of gray.

Look!
That break in the clouds.

Oh, how the light
Comes pouring through.
How beautiful
Contrasting
With dark shadows.

My Lord,
This beauty
Speaks so clearly
Of You,

Marie M. Constance

A reminder of Your presence
Behind the opaque events of life.

How sweetly You shine
Through hearts open to You.

Let me too
Be an opening
In the clouds
So Your light
Might find its way
Through my heart
To brighten the hearts of others.

I love You, my Lord,
My light,
My love!

"My Lord!"
Be assured of My constant protection. Hold her in My light and My love. Ask for truth, My dear, truth.
"Yes, Lord."
Peace, My dear.
"Lord?"
Yes?
"What of those who fear for her?"
Pray for peace and truth. Truth eliminates fear, and peace replaces it.
"Thank You, Lord. Take care of her, Lord."
I am.
"Take care of him, Lord."
I am.
"Take care of all of them, Lord."
I am. Take care of you, My dear.
"Hold me, Lord!"
I will. Concentrate on the cure, not the problem, My dear.

Living Reality

ങ്ക

Perhaps that desire
To be alone with my Lord
Was not out of love for Him
But an escape.

I could find so little spare time,
I thought I should give of myself
In that quiet place of prayer,
Our prayer room,
Any chance I could.

Now I think
He is really asking me
To let go of that desire,
To steal away,
To be alone with Him.

Instead I am to be with Him
Every moment
In action,
In silence,
In conversation,
In work,
In play…
Everywhere!

And I am to be attentive
To those I am with
And to their needs
At that moment.

To be present to them.

Marie M. Constance

For in being present to them,
I am being present to Him.

In serving them
I am serving Him.

When will I finally learn this?

This has been
His lesson for me
All my life.

When will I really learn?

It matters not when,
Only that I am open
To learning from Him
Every day,
Every hour,
Every minute.

No matter what He wants to teach me,
I want always
To be a true disciple,
To please Him
Just by surrendering,
By being,

Not looking for Him
Beside or behind
Or above or below
But here and now.

I do love You my Lord.
Let me prove my love to You.

Living Reality

I love You
Not for Your gifts
But for You, my Lord.

I love You.
I thank You for Your gifts,
But even when I don't feel Your presence
I still love You!

See Me in them so you might love Me in them.
"My Lord, when You say, *Talk to Me*, do You mean talk to You in them?"
Yes, My child. You are beginning to see the light. If you are attentive to their needs, you are attentive to Me.
"Remember when You said, *Find Me within*?"
Yes. That is the first step. And now that you know I am within you, you are going to learn I am within them too.
"I want to learn, my Lord. I want to learn from You."
You shall, My child. Just keep on listening for My voice and including Me in all you do, and especially in all your thinking.
"Oh, my sweet one, all You reveal to me is so wonderful. You are so wonderful, so generous, and so dear!"
My child, if only you knew how much I long for your love.
"Is it why we were created, my Lord? So we might love You? I hear no reply, only feel these sweet sensations in my heart, and tears. Oh my Lord, my love! Take my love. Take me."
I hunger for your kindnesses, your words of encouragement for these hurting ones. I long for your attention in them. Love Me in them.
"I want to be more aware. I want to know what to say, what to do for those in pain. Will You guide me?"
Remember that I am your guide. I am your strength. I am your love.
"My Lord, You are my all!"
Then live Me.

☙❧

Marie M. Constance

Oh my Lord,
Your hand on my cheek!

When can I see You
Face to face?
Yet even then
I would not be able
To look at You.

But I can feel You
Now
Without seeing You

So I ask not for sight.

Only increase
My abilities
To perceive,
To feel,
To know
Then to respond
More completely
In love.

Now, my sweet one,
Your hand rests
Not on my cheek
But upon my heart.

Such tender strains of love
Penetrate my heart
To its
Very
Core,
Wounding me

Once again
With the sweet,
Sweet pain
Of love's piercing arrows.

Oh, wondrous depth!

From this wound
I am bled
Of doubt.
I am cleansed.
I am whole.

"My Lord, tell me what You want of me today."
I want your presence, My dear, for those in need of Me because that is what you are: My presence to those around you.
"My Lord God, You are my all!"
Know that wherever your feet are, so are My feet. Know that wherever your hands are, so are My hands. Know that wherever your heart is, so is My heart. My dear?
"Yes, Lord?"
Know that the sweetness you feel in your heart is My caress. Feel My hand on your heart. Know I truly am holding your heart and all in it. Believe Me, My dear. It is Me.
"My precious God. This is what You meant when You said, *You will simply know*, isn't it?"
Yes, My dear. Come. Let Me increase your knowing as you let Me love you. Always, always it comes to one thing only: You love Me most, you please Me most simply by letting Me love you.
"My Lord and my God, then I am all Yours. Let me love You most and please You most. Now love me, Lord."
I am...I am...always...always...I am...

附옥

Marie M. Constance

I love You, my Lord,
Though so imperfectly,
So inconsistently
Do I attempt to prove
My love for You.

Yet Your love
Is constant.

Love me, Lord,
Though I forget
To love You.

I will remember
And try to make up for the loss,
But love me still!

That's it. Smile!
"I can't help smiling when You fill me with such sweet joy."
Then let me fill you more and more because I love to see you smile.
"Find Your pleasure in me. What an incredible wonder! What good, good news. If only all could hear that You are happy when we smile. Oh my Lord, let me bring You happiness. Spread Your happiness through me!"
So I shall, My happy child. So I shall. Come. Receive My joy. Here, first take My hand. Now come and receive. The incredible wonder, My child, is that many do not hear. I'm constantly trying to tell all this good, good news. Help them to hear.
"Show me how."
I am trying to show you every day.
"I am trying to learn."
Yes, you are. Thank you, sweet one.
"Another incredible wonder. You thank me! I know I haven't done all You have asked, yet You still thank me. You are a wonder, my Lord. You are wonderful!"

Living Reality

And I find you wonderful when you are so close, when you talk to Me thus. Stay close. Stay ever so close.

"I want nothing else, do I?"

You want to be close to your dear ones.

"Didn't You say You were, You are this longing, and You desire this closeness?"

Yes, but do you know what I want most of all?

"Tell me, Lord. Tell me."

I cannot.

"Then I know what it is. I long to be so purified of all desire, to cast off all other wants in one great, burning desire for You alone. This I shall do with all my will. I shall become all Yours, my Lord. I shall be Yours alone. I promise I will never, ever give up on this path to becoming totally yours. Never. I'm sure there will be slack times, but I will never give up."

This I long to hear and to receive, and I, My child, shall never, ever give up on you. Never. I have called you, and you have responded. So let us continue on your journey. Remember all I have told you. Learn all I have instructed. You and I shall have our want.

"I love You, my Lord!"

I love you, My child.

◊

My dear Lord,
I try not to dwell
On the sad happenings of war,
But I cannot help feeling
The plight of all who must suffer
Through this sadness,
This devastation.

I know it must be
Saddest of all
To You, my blessed, blessed one,

You who empathize,
You who know and feel
Every pain and sadness
Of Your people.
You who suffer with them
All the way.

Oh my Lord,
Let my love for You
Be of some use!

Show me what I may do.
I love You so.

Let go of all that. Come, we have universes to explore!
"My Lord, bless all who are struggling with life, bless them all! Oh, the sadness and pain in this world. Let Your blessings descend upon all and be a balm in all the strife."
I am, My dear, I am. You cannot see it, but I am blessing all. It is happening within, My dear, within.
"It is a beautiful day. I love to hear the birds singing. They seem to know something. Is it that spring is on the way?"
Yes, but you know that too, don't you? And I'm speaking of a deeper, bigger, fuller spring. Do you see that clearing over there?
"Yes, Lord."
That is what is about to happen in the world, My dear. There shall be a great clearing. Yes, a great clearing!
"My Lord."
The world is having labor pains, My dear. Labor pains.

ଓଃ ଓ

Oh, happy ecstasy,
The sweet embrace
Of God.

Living Reality

Oh, blessed wonder!

He, Lord of all,
Desires us,
Our attention,
Our conversation,
Our love.

He waits and waits
Until He can wait no longer
Then He floods one unaware,
Only to wait a little more
For that one
To turn to Him,
Melting,
To ask for more,

Delighting Him
By realizing
In joy
He is the one longing,
Pleading
To bestow love ever more!

Manifest, My dear, but this time manifest to Me.
"Oh, this is what I never imagined it to be. Suddenly I realize how I need to be needed."
Yes, My dear, and so do I. It is all so sweet, isn't it?
"Yes, my Lord. How very, very sweet."
That's what I intended, but with free will, things got kind of mixed up.
"They sure did."
Do you see now why I am so delighted when just one of My little ones realizes My love and My desire to love and fill, and then that same little one says yes? Do you see, My dear? Do you see?
"Yes, Lord, I see."

But there shall be more to see.

"I need to see only that You need me, and I need You, that You love me, and I love You. That is all I need to know, oh my precious, precious, wonderful God."

Come. Your pen?

"Yes, Lord. Forever and ever yes!"

Be motivated by love. Always let love drive you.

"My sweet, sweet Lord, Your love—oh, how wonderful is Your love!"

Now is the time, My child, to love with all your heart and soul, to love all in Me, and to let Me love all in you. As you come to Me, bring all with you and bring all to Me. Yet know that only in My love can you love all, for I am the love and I am the loving. I wish only to bring you into this loving, to love you in this loving, and to love through you in this loving. Do you see? My sweet one, let Me love you. Let Me then love through you, and then, My sweet child, love Me through this, My loving.

"I am at Your feet. I am in awe, in wonder, in gratitude. I am in love forever and ever with You. Show me how truly to respond 'yes!'"

Love...love!

Lesson Six: Remain in My Loving You

Let Me reveal Myself to you in this, My loving you.

Chapter Fifteen

Oh, to realize that my Lord and my God wants to reveal Himself to me in love! As in lesson three, in lesson six I am invited into a deeper and fuller understanding of His desire for me to live in a continuous state of being loved. Instead of saying, *Remain in My love*, He says, *Remain in My loving you*. There is a shift in emphasis, and though there remains a sense of being, there is also a sense of doing, as He explains He is actively loving me, and I am actively receiving Him.

In lesson six He explains that He is pleased when I get to the point of automatically thinking of Him because I am in love with Him. He longs for me to want to be with Him and to desire Him. When He is revealed in this way, as one who longs for me to receive His love and love Him in return, I just want to give to Him more and fill His lonely need. Oh, to know the need of God! He is certainly not one to ask for much. Rather He waits until I give and receive love freely, and then His delight is multiplied!

Just as He longs for me to let Him love me and then to love Him in return, so does He long to reveal Himself in the loving. I may come to know Him in this loving. I can't help loving Him more and wanting to be with Him and know Him more. There is automatic increase in both the giving and receiving as I know Him and His love more intimately.

On and on does He continue to bless and fill my heart with ever-increasing joy, awakening my soul as I learn to remain in His loving me.

I am so filled with gratitude! My God, so vast, so great, has become so close, so very touchable. I am in awe of His wondrous message of love and want to thank Him with all my heart and soul. My God has bestowed a treasure upon me, and how blind I have been at times not to see its all-glowing, all-shining brilliance. How incredible this is, yet how sweet, intimate, and close. How I want to please Him and respond, fully, with total surrender, with "yes!"

What a treasure to my heart is this love! I believe it will be here always, for it is from the eternal wellspring of love, the heart of my Lord. Such blessed warmth fills my entire being as I feel Him in this love and this love in Him. If only I could give Him all my heart and soul to thank Him for such love. Though this desire to give to Him rises spontaneously from within, how much time will it take to find fulfillment? Surrender to love may come in a moment but may take a lifetime to form and manifest totally. Though I yearn for such a moment and long to commit to a life of loving, the fear of time weakens my resolve to follow through.

Yet a sudden gift appears. How wondrous! In a flash I regain courage as He tells me to live in His eternal now. I realize that blessed moment may last through all eternity as I may live forever in Him. Blessed lover of all yearning souls, show me how to live ever surrendered to love.

I want to describe this that fills me, thrills me, and sends me. Such a sweet sensation flows in and around my heart as I write. When this sweetness comes, there is a tasting as well as a feeling, and a tingling not only in my arms, legs, and heart but almost everywhere, including in my mouth. I feel something flowing through me yet collecting me toward a center. There is a strong concentration of energy in my forehead and on the top of my head. The soles of my feet and my palms feel warm, and my fingertips tingle. My eyes are pulled toward the energy, my lungs feel clear, and there is a burning in my heart. Right now I feel a trembling. The more I attend to this sweetness, the more it increases in intensity, and the area expands. I think of Him and want to be totally His in this.

Living Reality

There is happiness in this sweetness that seems to be without condition, contrary to the kind resulting from fortunate events or circumstances. If I were asked to find a reason for it, I would say it is this sweetness I feel within. If asked to describe this sweetness, I would say it is this happiness I feel within, and I would just go around in circles, for each describes the other, each is in the other, and each comes with the other.

Why dwell so much on this? I think this sweetness combined with happiness is my perception of the indwelling Lord. This state of being is such that I am in joy, in peace, in love, yet in such a way that I am aware of another's presence in this with me, and at the same time I am in this other's person. It is as if the other surrounds me, envelops me, embraces me, and permeates me, yet this other is also next to me, distinct from me, and with me. I am in this other, and I am with this other. It seems as if the energy flows from this other in and through me and then around me. This energy carries with it the sweetness mentioned above, bringing me much delight.

How He fills me and consumes me in this great, burning love, this pyre into which I cast all desire but the one for Him alone. Into these flames I have also cast all fear of loving too much, for I cannot fear the life in my veins and my very existence. I can enjoy and rejoice in them. I am loving and receiving in and with the most incredible, wondrous love!

Such a wonderful one is my God! How He fills me day and night. As I write, the intensity increases, and I feel such blessedness of being here and now, with pen in hand. He is here. How I wish I could just place all my dear ones in this blessedness, this presence, this love. I am melting in the sweetness, the tenderness, the blissful, unspeakable knowing as He reveals to me once again, *I am this*. Oh, the sweet, sweet tears!

What a wondrous existence! Oh, this sweet fullness of being in such a wondrous place known as love. Moment-to-moment awareness brings increase, and occasional wandering from the presence, either in thought or perception, only makes the return that much sweeter.

He is all love and fulfillment. He is! Sweetly, gently, tenderly He carries me along on a most wonderful journey while in a most blessed wholeness, ever and ever wrapped (and rapt) in a wondrous embrace.

Chapter Sixteen

Sweetness beyond compare—
That is Your nature.

Oh, joy to be rapt
In You,
Though I know this is
But a tiny glimpse
Of You,
For I am yet weak
And not ready for more.

Make me ready,
Oh, my one!

Prepare for more, My dear.
"More?"
Yes, more of what I have in store for you. Do you recall what that is?
"Of course! Tremendous, wondrous, all-fulfilling love."

Living Reality

Yes. Here is how you are to prepare. First, be rid of all worries. I know of the things that worry you. I told you not to worry. I shall care for all your needs, even these. They are trivial.

"I have felt guilty.

There is no reason for that. You are doing your best. Leave it to My methods. They are far more productive than worry.

"Yes, Lord. I give these worries to You."

Good. Second, you must strive to keep your mind on Me. Do you recall the day I showed you how to let go and remain, and how to recognize whatever comes to distract your thinking from Me?

"Yes. I feel as if I've forgotten all You taught me already."

You just haven't learned yet. You are still learning, but My dear, I am pleased with your attitude and your desire to please Me in all aspects of your life. This enables you to learn faster.

"I marvel at this."

That's something else. Why marvel? All things are possible for one who is attuned to Me. So trust in this truth and be. I need your trust and your belief in My words and in yourself. Humility is tricky. Truly the humblest can see Me in all things, all persons, even in himself. Leaving all to Me, the humblest becomes My most faithful servant. So My dear, see My hand in your life, your molding, your unfolding, and your becoming.

"I'm trying."

The surest way is to let go and let Me, but your prayer enables My hand to guide. So pray without ceasing.

"Yes, Lord."

One more thing...

"Yes, Lord?"

Can you guess what it could be?

"Yes, I can."

Tell Me. Feel it, know it, and tell Me.

"Yes, Lord. You want me to be reborn every day. Every morning I am to awaken into Your embrace and tell You, as often as I may, all day long, that I love You, and I am to look for moments between activities where I may run to meet You and listen to Your voice and receive Your tender love. Then, at the close of the day, I am to fall asleep in Your arms and rest peacefully all night in your loving me. There is to be no separation ever, only varying degrees of attentiveness within and without depending on the matters at hand, and even while dealing with them I am to be thinking of You and receiving Your love. Is this close?"

Very close indeed. In simpler terms, My dear, you are to remain ever and ever in My loving you. There is more to this, isn't there, than My saying "remain in Me" or "remain in My love"? When you remain in My loving you, you are actively receiving as I am actively loving, and because I receive when you let Me give, I am actively receiving too, as you are actively loving. It is all the same. Do you understand?

"I think so."

This, My dear, is lesson six: remain in My loving you.

"With wondrous pleasure do I say yes to this!"

That delights Me. Come now. Are you ready to write as I prompt you?

"Am I ready, Lord?"

Yes. Proceed.

☙❧

    This morning I seek
    To know more deeply
    The love of my Lord
    By knocking on the door
    Of His dwelling place
    To enter in with humble devotion,
    Wrapped all in sweet memories
    Of being in that place before
    And joyful anticipation
    Of going there again.

My every heartbeat,
My every breath
Is a knock
Upon that door.

I rejoice as I hear
The voice of my beloved
Saying,
Come in.
The door is always open, My dear.

I want to reveal Myself to you, Marie.
"My Jesus, I feel Your nearness, Your love divine. I feel You are loving me now as I write."
Let Me reveal Myself to you in this, My loving you. Do not limit Me, Marie. Let Me be who I am. Let go of any and all preconceived notions. Let Me reveal who I am.
"Just lead me, Lord. I am Yours."
Come in, My dear precious one. Come in now, and let Me take over all you are with all I am.
"My Lord and My God!"
Come, Marie. I am waiting. How I want to reveal Myself.
"Jesus, I want the same. You must show me how to let You reveal Yourself."
I have been showing you, My dear. You have been receiving My revelations of love. Do you not know this?
"Yes, Lord. Yes!"
Then know I am this, this I am: love, love! Each time you enter My loving you, you receive more of My revelations of love. You know Me more each time you let Me love you, Marie. How I want to increase your knowing!
"Then increase it, Lord. Am I ready? Tell me what to remove if anything stands in the way. Just tell me. I shall let go."

You already have, My dear. You already have.
"Then what is in the way?"
Nothing, My dear. I simply await your entering.
"My Jesus, my lover, my only one."
There is one thing I want right now, My dear.
"Tell me, please."
It is simply your pen.
"Then of this too I shall let go."
Come, My dear. I await you in sweetest anticipation.
"You do?"
Yes. Believe and know this: I truly love you. I truly long to reveal Myself to you. I truly await you, My precious one, My dear Marie.
"Here is my pen, Lord."
I love you. Come.

☙❧

> My heart is full
> Of sweet tenderness,
> Of love blossoming.
>
> What a blessed state!
>
> I thank You, oh my God,
> For this.
>
> Help me do Your will today,
> For I can hardly contain myself.
> I can hardly concentrate on anything
> Save this wondrous feeling that tingles
> In my whole body
> But seems
> Especially centered
> Around my heart
> And in my forehead.

Living Reality

It fills me so.

All I want to do is love,
Love,
Love!

I cannot describe this with words,
Only attempts or suggestions.

I can almost taste something.

My tongue and throat tingle.
My eyes are heavy and feel tender.
My heart is on fire.
My spine tingles.

Yet all I really want to do
Is love
Tenderly,
Especially now,
Those who make tenderness grow in me
Because of affinity
Or bonds already established.

My Lord, this must be You

I bow to You.
I am at Your feet.

Use me
Somehow
For Your cause of love,
Even if it is to love
No certain individual
But all in You.

Just show me
How to love You
With this sweet tenderness,
With this awesome feeling
Of love divine.

I am Yours, my beloved.
Reveal to me Your wish.

How might I please You?

Receive my heart.
Work through me.
Love through me.
Love me!

My precious one, come. Give Me pleasure in your receiving My love.
"My blessed, beloved one, I am Yours."
Receive for yourself, My dear, and then share it. Share My love.
"Always, Lord, do I share Your love."
I know, My dear. I know. In this way My love goes out into the world through you. Hold the world, My dear. Hold the world and all in it in this, My love, in this, My loving you. Now, My dear, put away your book and your pen. Any words I speak now, keep them in your heart. If I wish any to be written, I will repeat them afterward. Come, My dear. Come!
"Yes, yes. Oh, yes, my sweet, sweet loving one."
Come. You must go deeper, My dear.
"Jesus, tell me what You desire of me now."
What I desire of you now, My dear, is you.
"In what capacity?"
In all capacities, My dear.
"Then all I am, I give to You, my Lord and my God, my eternal beloved."

Living Reality

Come to Me, My dear. I repeat: I await you.
"Do You still await revealing Yourself to me?"
Always, My dear. Come to Me, My precious. Come to Me now.
"My loving Lord, You are so tenderly loving always."
And always, Marie, do I await your receiving My most tender love. Come and love Me.
"Tenderly, Lord."
Feel My breath. I am this close...Your pen?
"It is Yours."

ଓଃ ଽଠ

Sweet, sweet, sweet
Is His caress.

His living love within
Does so fill
And inflame
Every fiber
Of my being.

Oh, to live
In blessed love divine!

My heart is
Melting.
My soul is
Flying.
My eyes are
Crying.

Oh, sweet salinity!
Oh, blessed, blessed love!

Marie M. Constance

The salty sting is only for
Love and longing
To be whole,
Complete,
One.

Yet oh, how my being loves to long.

What a delicious need
To want,
To desire,
To anticipate
My very own God,
Who says:

Come.
Love Me best,
Thus melting in Me.

Forever and ever
It is my desire
Thus to please
And love
By being.

By letting go,
And letting You,
My soul You are
Forever freeing.

What you feel right now, this very instant, My dear precious one, is My love filling you, is My tender touch, is none other than Me. I am the love. Always, always I am the love. Know Me in this love. Know Me in this loving. Love Me in this loving.

"Show me how to love You, my Lord, with all I am. Show me how!"

Come to Me tonight, My precious one. Approach Me with expectant joy. Greet Me with all the love in your heart. Come then to My heart in the fullness of your love for Me, and I will receive you, and you, My precious one, will receive Me. Purify it beyond words, My child. You know I love you.

When the pure thought of God
Settles in upon my heart,
It is as if
One drop
Of the most precious,
Deliciously fragrant
Oil
Enters my life stream,
Permeating my entire being.

Just one drop,
One pure thought
Of my God
Is enough to fill me,
Renew me,
Thrill me,
Consume me!

"I am so in love with You, my God, and oh, such a state to be so in love!"

Tell Me more, My dear. Tell Me more of this being in love.

"My heart is so happy in this state. I feel such a peace underlying it all. I also feel an intoxicating sweetness flowing throughout my being. I want nothing, only to be able to think of You and to perceive You in everything, to talk to You, to hear Your voice, to know You are here, to please You, and to love You. I want to offer You my very heart and soul. All this I want, my Lord, because I want You. Yet when I feel so in love with You, and I feel You are here, loving me in this love, I do not have to say, 'I want You' because, my wondrous one, I have You. Right here and now, I have You, and oh, the tenderness that fills me to overflowing. I love You, my God, my only one: You! Receive this, my loving You as I receive this, Your loving me. Oh, to give and receive at once. Oh, to be—yes—to be in love, where there is such an interchange, a blending, a flowing, a consuming, a melting, an enclosing, and a becoming one. Oh, breathless, deathless, endlessness, You, my God, only You. I enter You. I melt in You and become contained in You, yet I am uncontained expansion too, my Lord. In You I become You too. I become what I am in You, in love. Oh, blissful, everlasting God, my God, my beloved, my one forever. Yes! You, my God, are forever. This love is forever! In this do I too become forever?"

My love is forever, My dear. Yes. You shall understand more and more just what this means, but for now, keep telling Me of your love and of how My love pleases you. I find such delight in your words of love and in the strains of love in your heart. Delight Me, My dear, and tell Me every day that which I long to hear.

"Yes, Lord, every day. How I love and adore You!"

I love you too. Will you just call My name, if that is all that comes to your mind? Will you continue to call My name?

"My Lord, I love to call Your name. It is my favorite word, my favorite thought. You are my favorite thought."

Then indulge yourself, My dear, as you indulge Me. Finally you are getting to this point.

"What do You mean?"

I mean the point where we may be even closer because you are wanting rather than trying to think of Me. You think of Me because, as you say, you are in love with Me. For this I have been waiting! For this I have been longing, and now you are here. Oh, My dear, how pleased I am to receive this automatic loving, as you call it.

"It is automatic, isn't it? Whenever I have an instant to be alone, my thoughts automatically turn to You because I am so in love with You. Since You have made Yourself known to me, and because You are so irresistible, I love You more. If only all could know You so and grow closer to You in this knowing!"

You will help them know Me, My dear. You already are helping them.

"It is the highest privilege, Lord. I am so grateful for this blessing, for all Your blessings and all Your gifts."

I receive your gratitude, My dear. I receive your love. Come, let us love now. Come into this that I am. I love you, My dear. I love you!

☙❧

Love within me is not one-sided.
Both the giving and receiving
Happen within.

Whole is within me.
Not half
But whole.

Complete love He gives
Through me.
He receives in me.
He loves in me.

My heart is all aflame.

Oh, intoxication divine!

My heart is divine in Him,
Knows divinity in flesh.

Oh, blessed fires of love!

"Jesus, my Jesus, tell me that which You wish for me to hear. Speak, my most loving one. My heart is listening for the sweetness of Your voice."

My heart, too, is listening, dear one, for the tenderness in your voice.
"Really, Lord?"
Really. I do so long for your tenderness, My dear, and I receive any and all tenderness you give to others and even to yourself, for I am in all.

"My dearest dear, my very own, what an unbelievable wonder that You are mine!"

Yes, and I shall be ever and ever yours, My dear. Do you believe this?

"Yes, my Lord, I do, but it is difficult to imagine what that means, *ever and ever*. Though I hear Your words, and I, too, use these words, I do not really grasp their meaning. Faith is believing in things that are beyond meaning or understanding. You have given me faith. For this I am at Your feet in gratitude. I love You, Lord. How I long to love You tenderly, as You ask. My heart feels such sweet tenderness for You, but is this loving You? By feeling this tenderness, it seems as if I am receiving love from You rather than giving love to You."

Yes, when you feel this tenderness, it is Me. I am loving you, but have you already forgotten My message? To love Me you must let Me love you. To let Me love you, you must both receive My tender love and love Me with the same. Both the giving and receiving happen within. Do you recall using these very words?

"Yes, Lord."

Then know their meaning. In all loving, My dear, I am the love, I am the lover, I am the beloved, and I am the loving. As you realize this, you may bring more and more into this love. Come, My dear. Let Me take over your life!

☙❧

    Oh, the blissful presence
    Of my Lord!

    He comes,
    And He stays.

    Oh, how He stays!

Living Reality

With me,
In me,
Around me,
Through me.

Oh, blessed,
Blessed
Oneness.

He pulses through my veins.
He fills my lungs
With His very breath.

My heart beats in His.
My air is His breath.

He breathes
Life
Into me.

Life divine!

And fire!
He inflames my heart.

And water!
His love is liquid,
Flowing, filling, gushing.

And earth!
The very ground
I walk upon
Is His chest.

Marie M. Constance

The Earth
Contains His pulse.

His life pulses through.

And essence.
Oh, essence!

All is in essence:
My God!

His essence
Is in
All.

Sustains and renews
All.

All is one
In Him.

All is love
In Him.

All is joy,
All is bliss
In Him!

Oh, sweet tears
Release this essence
Overflowing
From within my being!

Oh, sweet release
then sweet return.

Living Reality

In and out.

Ever-flowing
Essence
Of my Lord!

Ever-flowing
Love
Of my God!

Oh, wonder
That He should come and stay,
Fill and remain.

It matters not where I am
Or what I'm doing.

He is here!

Oh, to be so enraptured
While doing,
While speaking,
While moving.

How incredibly sweet.
How very, very wonderful.
How very, very blissful.
How very, very Him!

No other words.

He is.
He just is,
And all is well!

"My Jesus, my beloved, My everlasting Lord. How You have filled me these days with Your sweet, sweet love, Your blissful presence, and Your wondrous peace. Such blessed, blessed peace can only be of You, from You, and in You. Oh my Lord, how You melt me in the fires of love divine. Oh, to know beyond any doubt this most wonderful truth: I am Yours, and You are mine. Everything else finds meaning only as it flows in and out of this one blessed, blessed truth: You and I, my God, are one. Endless thanks and praise be Yours, my Lord and my God, forever and ever. Amen!"

My dear, if you had not these words, what then would you give Me in their stead?

"My very heart, Lord."

May I have both? The words and your heart?

"You already have my heart."

Then what else will you give Me?

"What do You want, my Lord?"

I want all of you.

"Then take all of me. Tell me how I might give all to You. Tell me how I might please You more."

Here is how you may give all to Me.

"Why are You silent, Lord?"

This is how: in the silence. Just come to Me in the silence of your soul, and I shall show you how.

"Yes, Lord."

Now, My dear.

"Now?"

Now. Come.

"I am."

For this I have been waiting, My dear one. Why do you make Me wait?

"Oh Lord, I didn't know! I'm sorry to make You wait for anything I may give to You."

Then delay no longer. Come.

"Yes, oh my sweet one, Yes!"

Living Reality

☙ ❧

Oh, might You transform me,
My Lord!
Oh, take me into Your arms
And hold me.
Forever hold me,
Oh, my most beloved one!

It is You my heart craves,
You to whom my tears flow,
You in whom my soul rests.

Please, oh please, my Lord,
Draw me unto Yourself.
Take me in and keep me
Forever Yours!

Gently, gently do I lead you into all steps, all changes, all growth, My dear. I want to help you eliminate all fear. Do you believe I would lead you into something that requires your readiness if you are not ready?

"No, Lord. I guess I'm still distrusting my attunement to You and Your guiding hand."

Yes, and let's suppose that for one instant you let go of My hand. What do you think I would do?

"Reach out and clasp my hand again?"

Yes! And then what?

"Tell me, please, Lord. What would You do then?"

I would embrace you, My dear, and restore your confidence in Me that I am always with you. And I would increase your awareness of Me everywhere, and I would love you, My dear.

"So are You telling me I do not give You charge in the matter of my trust in Your constancy?"

I let you grow in this matter, My dear, but in order to give Me charge, there are times when you need to let go not of My hand but of the matter at hand. Do you see?

"I'm trying. You mean when things are unclear, unsettling, or even painful, still I should let go of the consequential matters, clasp Your hand more tightly, and let You lead me through it?"

Yes.

"But should I still try to work things out?"

Yes, but not alone! With and in Me is the only way.

"What else, Lord?"

You are still identifying with old patterns. These, too, you shall learn to give to Me, but I repeat, I shall lead you gently into these as well, as with all parts of this entire process.

"Thank You, Lord. Now I need to stop writing and go to the kitchen."

Yes. May I come along?

"Don't You always?"

If you let Me. Never let go of My hand wherever you go, whatever you are doing. This, too, is a way you remain in My loving you. Let this be.

"Yes, Lord. Keep loving me!"

It is truly My pleasure. Come.

Chapter Seventeen

The Beggar has come!

The Beggar knocks
Upon my door.

Asking, asking,
Please,
Please let Me,
Let Me give you more!

Unlike any other
Beggar known,
This one begs
Not to receive
But to give
All that is
His very own!

And as I do His bidding
(He says, *Let Me in!*)
There,

Here,
At the threshold
Does He linger
To show that He,
Though of essence divine,
Has chosen humbly
To transform His life
In reach of mine.

Breathing air as human,
This Beggar,
Unlike any other,
Begs and pleads,
Allow Me to love!
Allow Me to give Myself to you!
Allow Me to set you free!

Let go of all but the thought of Me. Feel My love. Let My love increase in you. Receive My love. Receive My devotion.

"Your devotion? I want to say, 'Receive *my* devotion.'"

Yes, but I am forever devoted to you, to all. I cherish you! Hear Me, My dear. Write this for all.

"Tell me."

I am devoted to loving all. I long for all to receive My loving devotion. You please Me, My dear, when you receive My love, when you let Me give you My grace and blessings, when you let Me love you. Oh, how I long for all to know Me as a loving servant.

"My Lord."

It is true, My dear. You have felt My tenderness when you've realized My service to you in little ways. You've felt My tenderness increase as you have received, haven't you?

"Yes, Lord, You are so very, very sweet."

Then taste Me forever, My dear. Taste My sweetness and let Me...

"What were You going to say?"
Let Me pour My sweetness over you and through you, and let Me fill you completely! Oh, My precious one, do not delay any longer. Now I want you for My own.
"You have me."
I love you, My precious dear.
"I know."

☙❧

How my Lord continues
To enrapture
My entire being,
Yet
In sweetness
Does He hold
My fragile heart,
In sweetness
And in promise
He will never ever leave.

Oh, this that fills me,
This that rises up
From within
My deepest deep
Center.

Oh, my very soul!

My soul rests,
Lives,
Exists
In this.

My soul
Is one
With this.

Oh, my pen
Wants to write:

"My soul
Is
This!"

Can I write so boldly?

Yet that is
What He tells me.

I am
Becoming
This.

I shall
Be
This
When I know
This
Completely,
Wholly,
As He,
As love.

As one!

Oh, to live
Forever
In this.

Oh, to die
In this.

It matters not.

I am His.

One
With Him,
In Him,
In this.

Forever
And ever.

Oh, blissful,
Sweet, sweet
Love divine!

I am well pleased with your being in love with Me, for that is your reason for living, your reason for being, My dear. It is to be in love with Me and in Me, and then you shall be this very love. One with me, one in Me, you become this that I am in you. I fill you with Myself. I surround you with Myself. Nothing exists apart from Me. I am all in all. I am...I am...I am!
"I know."
Yes, My precious dear, My Marie. Yes, you know.
"I love and adore You, my God."
I know.

ॐ

I rejoice
In such blessed anticipation
Of one
So intimate,

Marie M. Constance

So dear,
Coming in ever-new ways,
In ever-sweeter perceptions,

Oh, how my God
Sweetens all of life!

Taste the sweetness now,
Not the salt,
In my flowing tears
As they meander
As a stream
Warm and pure,
As they speak
Of only goodness
And kindness,
Of truth
And joy,
Of love divine
And peace eternal.

These tears must be mingled
With His tears.

Oh, sacred, sacred
Oneness
With my God.

My dear sweet child, I taste the salt in your tears.
"Oh my Lord, You are so sweet."
Cry your tears to Me, child, to Me!
"My Lord."
Share it with Me, child, with Me. Don't you know I long for you to make Me a part of your every experience? I give you experiences that you might share them with Me.

"Oh my Lord, I am sorry I forget. Oh, I am sorry. I long to share all with You, too."

Then do it. Cry your tears on Me.

"They are not sad tears."

I know what kind of tears they are. Give them to Me. Let Me taste the salt in your tears, especially if they are tears of tenderness, of love. Especially then!

"They are Yours, aren't they? Aren't they? I hear no reply—only increasing sweetness. Oh, increasing sweetness! My Lord, my God, oh my Lord, my love! I am here to love You. I am melting in this love that is of You and for You and from You."

Become this, My dear. Become this.

"I want to, Lord. What do I do?"

Nothing. Do nothing. Let go. Become. I will show you the way if you just once and for all let go.

"I'm trying."

Stop trying. Just be.

☙❧

    Oh my Lord and lover,
    Do not take this
    Sword
    From my breast.

    Pierce me
    Forever
    With Your love
    So sweet,
    So divine!

    Intoxicate me
    Forever
    With the wine
    Of Your presence.

Consume me
Eternally
With the flame
Of Your intense love!

Oh God,
Be my light,
My love,
My all!

"Sweet Jesus, another day of wonder. Thank You. Thank You!"

My little one, I am enjoying your joy. I find such delight in delighting you. Just be, My child. Just enjoy and be.

"I want to express my love for You every day and every hour, every minute, every second, every instant. Always, always, always do I want to give my love to You, oh beloved of my soul. Will You just let me know You are receiving this, my love, oh my dearest dear?"

My precious, precious Marie, I am receiving. I am! Oh, My dear, if only you knew. If only you knew how you delight Me. This is what I want you to tell Me, dear. Will you tell Me? Will you just let Me know too?

"What do You want me to let You know, my Lord, my sweet, sweet one? Tell me so I may delight You even more, for there is nothing I want more now than to please You. You! Oh, how I love and adore You."

I want you to tell Me you are receiving Me and My love, My dear.

"You know all things. Do You not know this as well?"

I want you to tell Me, precious. I want you to talk to Me about this that you feel. Tell Me how I melt you, for instance. Tell Me how I inflame your heart. Tell Me how you cannot contain so much of My love unless I show you how to let it overflow. Tell Me all these things, My dear. Tell Me your deepest secrets. Tell Me your deepest desires. Tell Me all you hope to find in Me, My precious. Tell Me so I may grant your every wish, so I may fulfill your every desire, so I may ease your every pain, so I may take away your every fear and make all your dreams come true. My precious, I long to be all you want, all you need, all you shall become. Come now, while we are alone. Come and talk to Me. Tell Me everything, and then in the silence give Me your all. In your telling, in your giving, in your sharing all you are with Me, I shall give you all I am as well. So, what do you say?

"I am already melting just thinking of this You so sweetly ask of me. Yes, Lord. Yes is what I say."

Good, My dear. How I love you. Come. Know this, My love, on this day set aside for love.

"Oh my precious, precious God."

My precious, precious dear, come.

"My Jesus, how it all makes sense. How everything relates to this one basic underlying truth: You love us and desire us. And it is just as true that we love and desire You! In this mutual yearning to love and be loved and this mutual desire to hear a profession of the same, You long to hear us tell You of our love for You and our desire to receive Your love. We long to know You love us, to hear You tell us of Your love for us and of Your desire to receive our love too. It is mutual. This mutuality, this longing is until we become one. You and each, each and You, You and all, all and You. Oh my Lord, my life, my all! Keep teaching me Your truth. Let me know Your heart. Let me know You!"

ଓଃ ଓ

Jesus, my Jesus,
Take me into Your heart.

It is there I wish to live
For the rest of my life,
Always and ever
Aware of You.

When I go within
And call upon You,
Such waves of joy
Flow through me.

Marie M. Constance

Every part of me
Is alive and afire
For You,
For the love of You!

Oh, sweet, sweet lover
Of my soul,
How can I ever thank You
For all Your
Wondrous gifts?

Almost daily now
You intoxicate me so,
And boldly I ask for more.

I've been told
You want me
To want You
Above all else.

It is in wanting You
That I am drawn to You
More
And ardently desire
All of You,
My Lord,
My God,
My all!

So take me now.
Make us one.
(We are one,
Always have been
And always will be,

Though I lack awareness
As I sleep
In not knowing.)

I doubt I could take
All of You,
My Lord.

Is that why
You
Reveal Yourself
In glimpses?

Each tiny glimpse
Sends me,
Thrills me.

I know not what to do.

What more can I take,
Though I still ask for more?

I am on fire
For You,
Oh my Lord,
My God.

I cry out to You.
Make me Your own!

I've been waiting for you, My dear. Are you ready?
"I don't know. I never know whether or not I am ready. I always answer You with 'I don't know' when You ask me if I am ready. Please just accept my yes in response to the other question You ask often as

well: *Are you willing?* Yes, my Lord, I am willing. Tell me if I am ready as well."

My precious dear, how you feed Me.

"Feed you?"

Yes, you feed Me with your yes.

"Then let me repeat it so as to feed You with my constant yes! My Lord, my life, my very existence, how You feed me. How I am nothing—lifeless!—without You but full and overflowing with life's truest essence, love, while I am with You and in You. Oh my Jesus, I die to taste You in me."

My precious one, come. Feed Me more, but let not the word yes be My next meal. Rather let the very essence you speak of be Mine as well. Share it with Me, precious.

"Then I am sharing You with You! Is that what You want, my God? Oh, to see and realize our very reason for being. To give You what You could not receive unless it is through us, Your created ones. Such blessed, blissful truth! This is why we have been created. You, the uncreated, absolute being of love and bliss, created us to receive and enjoy being in the oneness of love and loving with us. Oh, to glimpse this! You have let me see Your secret. You have let me taste Your need. My God, let me be Your beloved and share with You, my beloved, the preciousness of You. Oh, let me, show me how!"

Come, My dear. Let the secret unfold as you let Me enfold you. I love you! I desire you to be My own. Come, now.

"I melt as I feel Your arms enclose me. Oh, blessed, blissful being in love!"

My sweet one, My dear, My Marie dear.

"My Jesus, my Jesus, my love, make me Your own. Take me and make us one."

Come. Your pen?

"Yes, Lord. Take my pen as well. Always, always, always. Yes! Yes! Yes! How I desire You, my God, my Lord, my lover, You!"

Come.

⊛

Living Reality

My beloved Lord,
Purify my heart
In the love
You have awakened in me.

I want to love
You
With this love,
My dearest.

It is the only gift
I can give
To You.
You have everything else.

But You do not ask
For my love.

You wait for me
To give it freely,
Without reserve.

Here is my heart, my Lord.
Take it,
For it is Yours.
Forever Yours!

"Jesus, am I imagining what You are asking?"
My dear, such folly is this thinking! No, My dear, you are not making it up. I want this. I want this from you and in you and through you, Marie, My dear. I want you to be so filled with Me and My love that you cannot do otherwise.
"Do otherwise?"

You cannot do other than share this with Me. That is what I'm going to teach you, My precious: how to share this and give this to Me when you are so full. Now is the appointed time.

"My Lord and my God! Oh, my ever-living God, I am so happy about this. Thank You."

It pleases Me so to make you happy, My dear. Share your happiness with Me. Share your joy with Me. Share your all with Me, My dear. It also pleases Me when you share with Me that which you share with your dearest ones. Oh, My dear, let Me be your dearest.

"You are. You are!"

Come. Dance with Me in your joy.

"May I take Your hand?"

Please do. Come.

"Yes, Lord. Always, always, always: yes!"

֎

>Oh, how I yearn for You,
>My beloved God.
>How I burn
>With love for You.
>
>Tears flood forth
>From my soul.
>
>Receive this one offering
>I make to You tonight.
>
>My tears of love!

"My wonderful Lord, how my heart desires only You, forever and ever You!"

My dear child, come now as I have asked you to come. Let nothing stand in the way, My precious little one. Come to Me, and let Me fill you, for I long to give Myself to you.

"I long to give myself to You."
Then let us fill each other's longings.
"My Lord?"
Yes?
"Thank You for being so present all the time, so continuously present as love—sweet, blissful love."
You are right. I am love. I am bliss. I am sweetness, and the more you come to Me, the more I may reveal to you the very nature of love, My nature, Myself. I want you to know Me, My sweet one. I want you to know Me more so you might love Me more, and I might love you more completely as your capacity to receive increases. Come, My child. Come.
"I love You, my Lord. I love and adore You!"
Yes, you do. Now, put away your pen and do as I ask.
"Yes, my Lord, ask."
Your pen.

CR ɞ

Oh, love!

Love that fills my very heart
And soul,
Intoxicating me
I want naught else.

Only to love the one
Who loves me.

Reveal to me
Oh, lover of my soul
The secrets
Of the one true art.

The art of loving You!

"My Lord, my Lord, my Lord, I love You! I know not what else to say. It's all I can say to You now, for there are no other words to express what I feel for You."

My child, then say this and nothing more. Say this with your voice, your mind, your heart, your soul. Say it with all you are, with all your being. Say it with all the love I have given you! Say it and feel it. Know it and receive it, for I am this loving you feel. I am loving you. The more you receive, the more you let Me reveal to you. And the more you let go and be for and in Me, the more you are loving Me. So receive, enjoy, be!

"I am receiving. I am enjoying. Now show me how just to be."

Then put away your pen and come to Me. With all your heart, come to Me, and I shall make you be.

☙❧

> Sweet, shooting flames
> Suddenly pierce
> My heart,
> My eyes,
> My innermost being.
>
> Darting forth,
> Burning the centers
> Of devotion,
> Of seeing,
> Of knowing.
>
> Purifying,
> Intensifying.
> Oh, consuming.
>
> Only Thou
> Dost remain.

Living Reality

"My Jesus, my divine beloved, how Your love continues to hold me in a state of sweet, sweet bliss. How sweetly You have entered my being and filled me with love."

How sweetly you have entered My being and filled Me with delight, My precious one. Believe Me, My dear, believe Me. I find such delight in your happiness, in your contentedness in My loving you. Remain in My loving you. Actively receive! Let Me continue to make Myself known to you. Let Me continue to hold you in My embrace. Let Me continue to fill you with My very self. Oh, My dear, let Me continue to love you!

"Oh, my lover divine, such sweet ecstasy of being in You, in love with one so wondrously all satisfying, with You, my one and only one, my very own God."

My very own beloved, My Marie, My dear.

ଓଽଡ

Tonight, my Lord,
Let this writing
Be my prayer time,
My quiet time,
My alone time
With You.

Stay with me as I write.

I offer this time to You
And ask Your blessing
On me,
On my loved ones,
On all who seek
Your company
At this late hour.

Come, Lord,
Stay with me!

"I like being alone with You, Jesus."
You are alone with Me, My dear.
"I mean really alone."
And so do I mean really alone.
"Explain, please, my Lord."
You and I are one in each other. We are alone in this oneness. Our oneness is unique just as My oneness with another is unique. All are in Me. I am in all, yet each is one with Me uniquely. In this sense, My dear, you are alone with Me. Yet this aloneness is not loneliness, is it?
"Oh no, my Lord, quite the contrary."
Yes, quite the contrary to your thinking, I am alone with you now. You are alone with Me now. You may have Me, My dear, as I am now. I am alone with you in this, our oneness. Come. Know this. Know our oneness. Know our love. Know our aloneness, and thus know the truth.
"The truth?"
Yes, the truth.
"Explain, please, my Lord."
The truth that in knowing their unique aloneness with Me, all shall be freed of loneliness, the need to be loved, known, cherished, and the need to love, to know, and to cherish. In truth these needs are met and filled in oneness in Me. Do you see?
"I think so, but I shall return to these words again to realize their meaning more fully."
Return to Me! Return to Me, and realize My meaning in full.
"My blessed Lord, my lover divine. Already I feel the filling, my blessed, blessed God."
My blessed, blessed child. Come to Me as My beloved. Come to Me in this, our loving, My precious one, My dear.
"You melt me. You draw me. How can I resist?"
Don't try.

ಌ ಌ

Living Reality

I feel Your grace, my Lord,
Flowing through this pen.

My heart is sweetened
By perceptions of You.

Your love fills me
Then overflows,
Spilling over now
In the form of ink.

Oh, hear my prayer,
My Lord,
My beloved—

My prayer
That my pen
May always be guided
By Your grace,
My heart ever sweetened by
And this ink ever revealing
You!

My child, pick up your pen.
"Yes, Lord."
Tell Me what you are thinking.
"I am thinking this is all so incredible. I am thinking my life is so blessed. I am thinking You have been so constant in bestowing blessings upon me. In spite of my littleness, my lack of confidence as I try to stay, and my repeated falling into doubt and fear, in spite of all these obstacles I place on my own path, You continue to call me, to bless me, to love me beyond my wildest dreams! All this and more I am thinking, Lord."
So do you think it is but a dream? Do you think it is real? Do you think I am who I say I am, and do you think I tell you the truth?

"Oh, yes, it is real! Yes, You are my God! Yes, You always tell me the truth. You know when and why I doubt. You know, and You always rescue me when I cry out, 'Oh, hear and answer me, oh Lord, my God. Save me from myself!' Then You take me into Your tender love and hold me, refresh me, restore me to faith. Thank You for always coming to rescue me, yet there are so many, many blessings besides this for which I wish to thank You. And You have told me how I may thank You. Now, my Lord, I live to thank You, Now I live to let You love me and to love You and tell You of my love for You. For this I live."

Yes! That is the reason for your living, for your being, My dear. You live that I might love you. This is My truth, and you live to love Me, to talk to Me, to tell Me of your love. Yes, My dear, you live to love and be loved! There is no other truth more significant to your life. This is your truth because, My dear, it is My truth.

Lesson Seven: Balance

*I will come to you in your work, My child,
and I will come to you in your meditation,
but you must learn to balance your life.*

Chapter Eighteen

Just as in lesson two, where He encourages me to let Him make known the higher state of integration of body, mind, and soul, in lesson seven He points out my need to integrate. He leads me into understanding how I may remain with and in Him while at work, thus integrating action and prayer into increasing awareness of His ever holding and guiding me whether in the stillness of meditation or amid the business of life's daily demands. Learning to balance my life is the essential objective of lesson seven, yet fine-tuning that balance by attuning myself to His presence, and thus His will, is the higher goal.

It is wonderful to receive His counsel and encouragement while in the midst of activity. Yet as I continue to converse with Him, I am so often filled with love and in such awe that I know not what to do. Fortunately there's enough housework for me to do that I don't need to look far to find ways to integrate. But while I walk around this house, little does anyone know I am really swimming in a sea of love. Oh wonder, oh joy, oh sweet, sweet being in love!

When experiences in this life with Him increase in intensity, if not for His watching after me, I would have a tendency toward imbalance. I might neglect to eat properly or get enough sleep except for His pulling me back to solid ground and practicality. For instance, once, after an experience of feeling others' pain (which is what He told me I was feeling), I brought that pain to Him and pleaded with Him to take care of them.

He replied, *Take care of you, My dear.*

Feeling so drawn to Him, a few times I stayed up all night to remain awake in His presence. Yet on another night, with the opportunity and longing to go without sleep, I made the assumption He would want the same. Instead He told me to go to sleep and be with Him in sleep! Once, when I thought I should be fasting for a certain prayer, He told me, *I want you to eat. I want you to stay nourished. You may fast another time. Now I want you to eat.* I remember one evening not wanting to eat because I had just seen pictures of starving children on the television, and since I was home alone, I thought it would be a good offering to skip a meal. He told me to eat and receive nourishment for those children!

Even knowing when or when not to pick up my pen requires a sense of balance, yet if I attune myself to Him and simply ask, He graciously lets me know the right course. Though conversations with Him are often short and sweet, sometimes deeply intimate, sometimes instructive, sometimes just gentle reminders, they are continuous in the sense that He is always here. As soon as I call His name, He answers, and oh, how my heart fills up!

Sometimes it is as if my pen is called to take a break from recording the conversations we have. As I think about it now, I see those breaks as a sifting time when He asks other things of me, when writing has to wait. Afterward He reminds me of my need to write His words for future reference. When He instructs me to come, I melt as I glimpse understanding. I melt as I feel such sweetness permeating. I fly as He carries me oh, so high into His blissful self, into love.

Once, during a time of struggle, I knew I had been lacking meditation and deep prayer, or entering. Then I received His command: *You must come deeper. This is what you need: to come deeper.* Once again He blessed me with the reassurance that only He can give in His presence as peace. Another time while praying, I said, "Convince me, Lord. Convince me it is You!" Immediately a wave of tingling energy and sweet love permeated my entire body. I cried. Oh, so sweet is my lover divine!

Living Reality

In another instance I felt an increase in the intensity and pull of love, so I proceeded to write a conversation beginning with, "I need to talk to You now, my Lord." He followed with a clear message that He had something to reveal to me if I would go deeper. I felt as if something bigger were coming my way, so I knew I had to heed His call with all my will. I reread the conversation with Him and proceeded to try to go deeper.

In the initial stages there was no resistance, but as time went on, believe it or not, a struggle came that made me wonder what was going on. Then I just let go of the struggle and, directing my thoughts to Him, asked for help. It was so nice because I then realized the nature of that struggle. In imagining something bigger, my approach had been different.

Then and there He said, *It is Me. It is Me. You need not try so hard to prepare yourself for anything or anyone else. It is Me. Stop trying so hard.*

I realized I had been struggling with something of my own making. He showed me He asked me to go deeper only so I might know Him more completely, and I had been trying to do more than that. He helped me let go and just relax in His sweet presence. What a wave came over me! I felt so comfortable with just Him. That's all it is ever about anyway, is it not? Just Him? What a blessed comfort as I felt Him more personally then and all day. After the struggle was over and peace returned, I remained in the quiet a little longer until He told me to pick up my pen, although I had been thinking I had to learn to put down my pen. How often He has turned my conclusions around. I thought I was not yet ready to resume writing, but He said I was. Then oh, what followed!

The sweet level of comfort I feel in His presence makes it easier for me to receive His teachings on balance. And much like any loving parent, by first establishing a foundation of love and assurance, He may then teach through example. He is not only reassuring but very courteous. I remember once being a bit surprised by the way He showed me great courtesy when I had expected a more casual reply from Him. He asked why that surprised me so and told me to follow His example by always being courteous, especially with those dearest to me.

On several other occasions, He suggested I follow His example, yet He was never demanding or reprimanding. Instead it was very characteristic of Him to be humorous first before showing me my mistakes or folly. He often caused me to laugh aloud or to smile broadly in response to some play on words or some witty comment about matters in discussion. By turning situations around quite dramatically, He showed me the folly of taking myself too seriously. For example, while driving home from work one day, I was thinking about His telling me I needed to work on balance. Just as soon as I prayed, "Lord, keep me balanced," six or seven cats strolled merrily across the street in front of me. I laughed aloud at such a sight!

Then I heard His response to my laughter: *This, My child, will keep you balanced: your sense of humor. Always keep it alive.*

On another occasion, while walking by the sea, I was surprised by the outcome of His interrupting my thoughts. He said, *Do you know who I am? Do you really know who I am?*

As I gazed out across the ocean, I began to feel who He is.

He then said, *You must come into the stillness to know who I am. To know who I am truly, come into the stillness, My dear.*

I said, "I will, Lord. I will come into the stillness, but do I have to wait? Can't You just reveal Yourself to me now, while I'm here?"

Then oh, the sweetest love and light flowed through me in a continuous wave! I stood still; I gazed out across the ocean, where the sun's light was reflecting so beautifully on the water. He held me in that beauty, and I knew it was my God.

Once, when I had been longing to find a way to deeper quiet and prayer, I realized so many opportunities for these things had already come. For instance, He had gifted me with three days in a row of being near the ocean. What a supreme gift. All seemed clearer just by my being in the ocean's vicinity and blessing. I saw new ways simply to be in a deeper state of quiet even in the midst of activity. When the opportunity for solitude came, I realized that in the knowledge of His constant presence, both activity and solitude can nourish and renew the soul by filling the need to be.

Living Reality

After visiting the ocean, He showed me I did not need so much time in solitude to go deeper, or to find stillness and be in that stillness. Rather I was already in such a place. I was in Him then already! The need I had been feeling to find solitude and stillness was real, but He helped me see I would be able to do so quickly and often, and the goal—Him—would always be attainable. I would not need to go anywhere, and even if depth would be needed, the way could be simpler and fuller by the gift of His sweet, sweet presence, so constant.

I understand that my goal now is not to find more time for deeper prayer but to be more constant in awareness that He is here, and I am in Him. When those few moments or hours (gifts!) come as opportunities to give myself to Him in quiet, depth, and stillness, I will see and respond. All will be clearer as I continue staying in Him no matter where I am, what I'm doing, or who else is near, ever striving to find my equilibrium in Him.

Chapter Nineteen

It seems a monumental task
To balance my life
When my heart is not attuned to You
Or earnestly seeking You.

Yet the task becomes
So very light
When all is done
With the thought of You
Uppermost in my heart.

Oh, to be ever and ever
Attuned to You!

My most earnest desire
Is never to lose
My love and longing
For You.

May the flames
In this heart

Ever grow,
Burning away
All but the one desire
For You, my Lord,
Only You!

"My Jesus, what is next?"
Lesson seven, My dear. Do you want to know what it is?
"Already I hear the word, my Lord."
My word. Yes, My dear. Balance. This is lesson seven. Hear Me, My dear, and rejoice that you hear Me.
"I am rejoicing. I've been celebrating!"
Celebrate with Me. Rejoice with Me. In all you are, be with Me.
"Yes, my loving Lord, always yes. Can we begin now?"
Yes, let's begin anew. Come. I will come to you in your work, My child, and I will come to you in your meditation, but you must learn to balance your life.
"If I come to You now and breathe in Your name and dive into Your oceanic presence, and then afterward will You help me get my work done?"
First of all, My child, see how you separate diving and praying from action and work? Do not separate. Strive to unify and live in Me always no matter what you are doing. Second, My child, it is not your work but My work. Remember it is all My work. You are My instrument. If you truly empty yourself so I may fill you with Myself, you will be My channel, and you will know My will.
"Now, Lord, I will empty myself so You may fill me, and I will swim in You all the time and love You in the swimming."
Yes, My dear one, love Me…Now for the emptying.
"I am Yours, my Lord. Take me and fill me!"

☙❧

I am prompted
To write of You,
My dear Lord,
Prompted by Your love.

Your love is so strong,
I need to let it flow
Through.

It seems
The more I let it flow,
The more keeps coming.

Such is true of Your nature.

The more love is given,
The more love grows.

It does not diminish
It is not used up.
It grows and grows and grows!

"My Lord, my dear Lord, good morning."
Know the things I ask of you are also in My will for you. Do not resist. If I told you I gave you this time for this purpose, then follow My will. Yes, you will be able to keep a balance if you follow My will, which is perfectly balanced. Resist not the role I have given you. See whatever I require of you as an integral part of your daily life. You may have and live several roles at once, and each may be integrated with the others. There is a balance, My dear, and I shall help you find it. Are you willing?

"Yes, Lord. Yes! Just lead me and show me the way. And help me discern."

I am leading you. I am showing you the way. I am discernment. Relax, My dear. All you have learned is leading you in My grace, yet all the while I am holding you in My tender embrace. All the while I am loving You. Remain in this, My loving you, and all the rest shall follow.

"Oh my Jesus, my most blessed lover divine!"

My dear?

"Yes, Lord?"

Living Reality

I hear all your thoughts, My dear. I hear all your prayers. Writing is a means to My blessings. Haven't I told you this many times?

"Yes, Lord."

So is rereading a means to My grace. All you hold in your heart receive as you receive—while you pray, while you write, while you reread—because these all contain My grace. You are in Me all the while, just as you remain in Me while you perform your work. All is in Me. Do all in awareness of this truth: I am in you, you are in Me. Always, always, always. Let Me bless all, no matter what you are doing, through and in you, My dear. Hold all in this.

"Yes, Lord. Forgive my separating."

Integrate. Let all flow as sweetly as the soft summer rain.

☙❧

Now, help me, my beloved
To go to work
In service to You
In my family,
In my friends,
In whomever You place before me.

You intoxicate me so
With the wine of Your presence.
Drunk with Your love,
I know not what to do
Or how to perform my tasks.

Yet You come to me
In my duties
As well as my prayers.

Keep me ever aware of You
While I work or play,
Sleep or pray.

Awaken me
Into ever-increasing awareness
Of You,
Only You!

I wish to tell you something now.
"Guide my listening please."
Fear not. I always guide your listening and your writing. Proceed. Your life, My child, is My gift to you. You know this, don't you?
"Yes, Lord."
So is life My gift to all. Life is to be treasured and lived in such a way that awareness of its worth is made manifest. I want you to live in this way, child.
"Please explain more."
Now I wish for you to think of and understand this. Now I wish for you to understand this. Now I wish for you to live this. Eliminate unnecessary activity and the accumulation of things that dull awareness. You will know, child. I guide you ever on this path. Simplify as best you can. Always strive for moderation and balance. Above all cherish life, cherish My gifts, cherish each other. So shall your awareness of My blessings increase, and so shall those around you grow in the same awareness. Live in My love, My dear. Live in Me.
"I love and adore You, Lord. Thank You!"
No matter what you are doing, My dear, be assured you are ever in My embrace. If you are occupied with activity, rest in the certainty that I gave you this activity. If you are occupied with writing, rest in the certainty that I desire this as well. If you are drawn to quiet prayer, then by all means, come! Let go, My dear, and let My hand guide you in all things. Sweetly, cheerfully, peacefully, and contentedly follow My lead always. Plan as little as possible, My dear, and you shall see My hand at work in all aspects of your life. Oh, My sweet little one. Let go and let Me.
"My dear, dear precious Lord and friend, take my hand now, and lead me wherever You will!"

☙❧

Living Reality

When I finally started
Washing the dishes,
I felt a wave of sweet joy
Flow through my being.

He seemed to be saying,
*I've been waiting for you
To do dishes with Me.*

Then a smile swept across my face,
And my heart was pierced
By yet another arrow.

I've been told
We find our God
In the everyday circumstances of life.

How wonderfully true!

Not only do we find Him
But we receive and enjoy Him as well.

Oh, come and stay with me,
My dearest, most beloved friend!

"My Jesus! All I want is You, to please You, and to know I am pleasing You."
Then you have all you want.
"Show me what You want, Lord."
I want you, My dear, to be ever and ever enraptured by My love.
"Then show me how to give You what You want."
Receive, My dear. Receive!
"Help me to let go. I need Your help right now in letting go."
My precious little one, I receive your tender tears now. Know I always taste the salt in your tears. I know all your longings, My dear. Won't you just tell Me about it?

"Yes, Lord. That is it. I wasn't talking to You. I was just thinking to myself."
Come. Let's get back to your kitchen. You can tell Me all about it while we work together.
"My dear, dear tender loving one, my sweetest, sweetest one, how I love You!"
Me too. Come now, to your dishes. We can dance while we do them.
"You make me smile."
That's why I said it. Keep smiling. It will spread like fire!

☙❧

My Lord
I want to give You my heart,
Dear one,
Not later, not tomorrow,
Not next week
But now!

Receive my heart
With all its imperfections.
Receive me now.

Take me into the shelter
Of Your heart
So warm,
So tender,
So pure,
So wonderfully wonderful!

I know I have so much to work on
In striving for purity,
For perfection.
It's hard even to think
Of striving for such,
Let alone getting there.

Living Reality

But if I keep my eyes on You
Instead of on me,
I will go where You want me to,
And I will hide myself in Your cloak.

There will be no room
For fear or cold,
Only shelter
And warmth
And happiness
Just to be with You.

So each day
I place myself at Your feet
And ask You what You want of me.
All I seem to hear in response is,
Your love, My child.
Your love!

Then receive my love
As it is now, my Lord,
And I will wait no longer
For my love to become better
Or more pure.

Take all I offer You now,
My dear, dear Lord,
And make me Your own.
And then show me
How to love the flowers—
My dear ones
You have given me.

As I place them at Your feet,
I ask You

To bless them daily
With Your
Life-giving light
And Your living water.

Sustain them each and all,
My dear one,
And sustain me.

Fill them with Your love,
Your joy,
Yourself.
And make us all one
In You
Forever and ever.

Amen.

I hear and answer your every prayer, child. Believe this. Ask, My child. You do not offend Me. I know all things, but I wait for you to ask.

"Sometimes I feel as if it is best to be silent, or to say, 'Because You know all things, You decide.'"

I have taught you the way to bring those in your prayer to Me when you are still, and it is best for you to enter first. But at all other times, ask. When you are talking to Me, ask. Do you see the difference?

"Yes, Lord. In stillness You want me to let go of thought processes and go deeper. In activity You want me to keep in constant communication with You, to give my full attention, if necessary, to the task at hand so as to do a good job but give attention to You when the job is done."

You may also give attention to Me while you are giving attention to the work.

"Explain, please, Lord."

Living Reality

Give Me your heart before you begin a task. I know you would rather talk to Me than to others sometimes. Yet if you give Me your heart before, and then your attention is fixed on the task, you are still being attentive to Me. Remember you are working for Me in all you do no matter how small the task. And you are serving Me in all you serve no matter how small or lowly. I am in all! Just enjoy the rhythms of this day.

"Yes, Lord."

Be at peace in this luxury I have bestowed upon you.

"Explain, please."

The luxury of refocusing in the setting of your home, My dear. Many cannot do this. It is a luxury for Me too that you should listen to Me, love Me, and let Me love you. Many do not give Me this.

"I do not want to seem ungrateful. I know You have given this luxury to me. Please, help me make good use of it, and let it not be at the expense of others, especially my family and any I may be called to help in another way in this time."

My dear, do not think you are not helping. Do not measure in those standards that measure by outward results seen and felt. I am calling you to a higher service within. Yes, fulfill your obligations daily, but do this in Me. Remain in Me, and do all things well and cheerfully, as if you were playing with Me all the while. When you feel resistance, see it as such and give it to Me. Meet all things with a spirit of willingness. I shall supply you with the energy and the balance. Do not fear.

☙❧

I feel as if I could go on
Forever
Writing, singing, thinking
Praises to You,
Yet I know eventually
I will slip away,

Marie M. Constance

Only to come back to You
Again.

Oh, for the day
When I'll never slip away
From You again,
When I remain ever and ever
Locked in the chains of Your love,
Never to leave You
Ever again.

Melted in Your bliss
Forever and ever.
One,
Oh, my own.

All I am
I lay at Your feet.

Take this offering,
My sweet one,
Then show me Your will!

"Blessed Jesus, I've been waiting all day to write with You."
I've been waiting all day for you to come to Me.
"I have been trying to do as You said, Lord, to come to You even when we are not alone. I was not alone with You at all today. I talked to You as often as I could while in the car. What do You mean You have been waiting?"
Waiting for you to give Me your heart.
"How, Lord? In what way? Please explain."
Be more deeply conscious of the act of giving Me your heart. Do not just say, "I give You my heart." Rather, feel that you are giving Me your heart. Feel and know it.

Living Reality

"Sometimes I say it but do not feel it because there are others around."

Learn to do this no matter who is around, child. You can do this. I want you to do this.

"Oh my Lord, I want to. Show me the way."

Visualize this. Say My name. Call upon Me. Offer Me your heart. Do you know what it means to offer Me your heart?

"I thought I did, but I wish You would explain it and make it clear to me."

That means you must give Me everything that is dearest to you. It may even mean your security in the person you believe yourself to be. I want you to see what I see, child.

"What do You want me to see?"

You are not a meek, silly child. You are My dear one. See yourself as dear to Me, and then, when you give yourself to Me, know you are thus dear to Me. Give yourself to Me in love. You know how.

"My Lord, My dear Lord. I am so sorry for not understanding and for not realizing. I am speechless now, for I am beginning really to believe and see that You mean what You say, and I am dear to You! Oh my Lord, let me make up for all my folly by truly loving You with all I am, with all that is dear to me. I want to let go, to give all to You, to hand it all over and thus melt into Your being. Oh my Lord, I am sorry for my lack. I want to love completely. Forgive me, and receive me as I am though my offering is incomplete."

For this I have been waiting all day.

"Why didn't I know?"

This is another step. Listen more carefully, and you will take more steps.

"I did call upon You all day long, as You instructed."

Yes, but call not only with words in your mind. More so, call Me with your heart.

"I thought I did. Thank You for revealing this to me. I want to get closer to You in whatever way I may."

Your heart holds the secrets, child. Keep your heart ever attuned to Mine.

"Show me, Lord, from moment to moment. Show me the way."

Marie M. Constance

My name, your heart. Remember this, dear one. Love Me thus, and you shall not only get closer, but you will know what I have told you. We are one. Realize it and live in it. Oh, My child, My dear child.
"I love You, Lord. I do love You!"

⚭

Oh Jesus, my Jesus,
Why am I so restless?

My heart fills up
With love,
Then I know not
What to do.

I know I must
Go deeper
And deeper
Truly to find You
And let my soul
Rest in You.

Yet oh, this love!
How it lifts me so,
How it stirs my heart
And prompts me to love.

I want nothing else
Than to feel Your love
And then turn
With this love
To love others.

Show me how,
My Lord,
My dearest.
Show me how!

"My Lord, I was restless, so I felt perhaps I needed to write what stirs within me. Now I pick up my pen, and the only thing I feel inclined to write is: 'What would You have me write?'"

I've been waiting for you, child, not only to prompt written words but to hold you when you come to be alone with Me. This I ever await.

"Do You also wait for me to be more attentive to You while I'm not alone with You?"

When you are with others, attend to them. Personalize your attention. When you are not with others, love Me with all your heart.

"Do I do this already, Lord? I try to."

Yes, but still your thoughts wander. The more centered you become, the more I am able to bless you and those around you. Why do you hesitate and busy yourself so?

"Because there are so many things I think I am supposed to be doing, I think I should do something first and then write because writing is such a pleasure. Sometimes I feel it should follow duty."

You see how your attitude is going back to your old way of separating? That is why you call these things "duties." Think of them rather as acts of love, My dear, and all shall flow so sweetly. Concern yourself with the one thing I have asked you to do. All the rest will come and will flow out of this.

"Tell me again, Lord, what You want me to do."

Stay in Me. Remain in this. This is My love. Receive this. Be in this, and let this flow through you into the world. Restrict not the flow with your worries, doubts, and fears. Be in My peace.

"Yes, Lord."

If you let Me love you in this, you shall bear My light to the world no matter where you are or what you are doing. I know you have little faults and failings and weaknesses. Trouble yourself no longer about these. These are meant to keep you humble. If you were perfect, no one could bear to be with you.

"You are so sweet."

I know.

"I love You, Lord."

I love you, My dear. Will you allow Me to say your name?

"Of course."

I love you, Marie, My dear.

"Lord, You fill me so!"

Good. Let it overflow. Do you hear that sweet, little bird singing?

"Yes."

He feels it too, you know. That is why he sings so sweetly.

"How nice."

Yes, how nice. Now, place all your cares in My hands. Yes, you may also place your dear ones in My hands. Now.

"Thank You."

It is truly My pleasure. Now you must go to work. Remember: remain, receive, be open. Let Me love you!

"Yes, Lord, a thousand million times: Yes! Yes! Yes!"

Come. Take My hand.

☙❧

> As I drove through the woods today,
> I became so intensely aware
> Of Your presence, my God,
> In all my surroundings—
> The sweet sunlight reflecting
> Off the green, green leaves,
> And that wonderful blue
> (Your eyes)
> Of the sky shining through.

Living Reality

I asked You to tell me of Yourself
As Your love filled me so.

Your answer came
Through my feelings
Of loving.

I felt such an intense desire
For my loved ones
To receive
The love I perceived
Going outward
In their direction.

I didn't really feel the desire
For them to love me,
Just for them to let me love them.

Then I knew.

You are like this,
My God.
You long for us
To let You love us,
To receive all You wish
To bestow on us.

It is wonderful,
My God—
Almost too good to be true.

Yet I believe
You showed me
This truth today.

Never let me forget this,
My dear,
Loving God.

Now, if it pleases You,
Love me!

"Jesus?"

Yes, My dear?

"Why is it that I cannot remember what You said to me a little while ago, though I do remember thinking, *I should write this down later when I get a chance?*"

It is not required that you remember what I said or that you write it down. It was meant simply for the moment in which it was spoken. Relax, My dear. This shall happen frequently, and you are not to be concerned in the least with your not being able to remember it all. OK?

"OK, Lord. Thank You. Anything else?"

Tell Me how you feel when you listen to My saying your name. Tell Me now.

"I feel so loved, and this feeling of being loved by You is so very soothing, so filling, so calming, so affirming, and so sweet, Lord, oh, so sweet! I listen for that which makes this so uniquely You, and I feel so highly blessed to be able to hear this. To hear Your voice at all is incredible. Oh, to hear Your voice saying my name so tenderly, so lovingly, so sweetly, so intimately, so dearly, so pleadingly and longingly. How can it be? But it is. It is true that You, God, long for my closeness, so I am close enough to hear Your voice whispering my name. It is beyond belief at times, but I do believe, Lord. I do!"

Thank you, My precious, for telling Me this, for writing this. Others will benefit from your words about Me and My desire to be close enough to be heard, even in a whisper. Yes, many shall realize My longing for closeness with My people is constant. They shall see this through your eyes and heart, your writings, and your prayers. Then, My dear, they shall be better acquainted with Me and My truths, with who I am. This is why I say thank you to you, My dear Marie.

Living Reality

☙ ❧

My Lord,
Dearest beloved of my heart,
Of my soul!

What is this plan of the Father?

In this life,
So full of uncertainties,
One great constant
Always remains,
Forever *is*:
His love
For all His creatures,
His love
Through You,
Through the Spirit.

So much has been taught,
So much I believe,
Yet what do I truly know
Through my soul's
Awakening?
Through Your constant
Blessings?
How receptive am I really?
How much is
Only in my mind
And not truth,
Absorbed by my being
Or awakened
In the light of Your loving presence?

Marie M. Constance

When I am
Full of love in my heart,
Full of joy in my whole being,
Aware of and excited about You,
Feeling that blessed closeness,
Or, better,
Unity
With another,
Then doubts dare not
Enter my mind.
If they try
They are shoved away
By the sheer force
Of the love alive.

Yet when circumstance
Or neglect—
Whatever the cause—
Enters and disturbs the peace,
Then what, Lord?

Doubt comes, and questions arise.
Confusion sets in,
And then moods take over,
Upsetting the flow of love.

Relationships suffer,
Duties are a struggle,
Patience is gone.

Where do I go astray?
How can I learn to stop this
Before it takes over?

Living Reality

It seems I keep falling
Into the same pit of delusion.
What is the key,
The solution?
Is the key the very one
You have offered?

Yet how often do I turn away
And say, "Not today"?

Oh, my Lord,
Do not measure my love for You
By my lack of consistency
On this path I travel.

Rather, Lord,
Measure my love
By my unwillingness to give up
Though I meet countless struggles
Along the way.

Though my heart
Is not always feeling
Love and yearning for You,
You know
I will never stop
Looking for You,
Looking for Your love
And for ways to love You.

So often, amid the distractions
Of daily life,
I forget to talk to You
Or think of You,

Marie M. Constance

But then You surprise me
In some little way.
You are still with me.

Thank You, my Lord,
For all Your wondrous blessings.
I hope I may please You more.

With Your blessing
May I discover Your love
In new ways.

Help me
Not to forget so often
But to remember more!

I do love You, my Lord.

I write this to help myself
When times are tough.
I know You hear my every
Thought and prayer,
Yet for my own benefit
I write some down
So I may have hope
In times of trial.

Again I am at Your feet,
Asking Your blessings
For my loved ones,
For those in need,
For me.

Help me better serve You

In those in my care—
Really in Your care,
Yet You do use me.

Let me never forget
You are the doer, not I.

I am Yours, my beloved,
Now and forever.
Amen!

"Teach me the right attitude to have toward life's experiences, my Lord."
Listen. Always listen for My voice. I will guide you always on this path that leads to Me. Yet when you meet with obstacles or confusion, see these as steps to your goal. To cross over the hurdle is to become that much closer to the finish. To deal with confusion is to clear the way for more understanding. Above all, My child, realize I am with you in all your experiences. Keep talking to Me. Keep telling Me of your love, and nothing shall prevent your glorious finish, your freedom, your liberation. I am your teacher. I am your guide. I am your companion. I am your Lord. Know Me in all these, and continue to come to Me as My beloved. You are My beloved. You are precious to Me. You cannot even imagine how great My love is for you. That is why I say, "Come to Me." Let Me reveal Myself to you. Let Me love you. You will not have to imagine. You will know.

"Oh my sweet Lord, I thank You with all my heart for such sweet counsel. For all You tell me, my Lord, thank You!"

It is My delight to instruct you, to guide you, to hold you, to welcome you into being, to awaken you into knowing, to receive you into loving.

☙ ❧

My Jesus,
My Jesus!

Marie M. Constance

You are so
Wonderfully present
In the most
Unexpected ways.

You are
So full of surprises
That delight my soul!

Do You,
Oh blessed one,
Take delight
In blessing us this way?

I feel Your smile, my Lord.
I feel Your joy, my sweet one.
I feel Your love, my beloved.

Now, show me how to smile,
To bring joy,
To love.

Stay with me, my Jesus,
And show me how.

My Jesus,
My Jesus,
My love!

My dear, continue, no matter what you are doing, to breathe My name. In this way I shall help you calm yourself, and you shall find patience as you feel My peace.
"Then come with me now, Lord."
I never leave your side.

"Already Your peace is settling over me and flowing through me. Don't stop now!"
Be assured. This is only the beginning!
"How Your smiles give me balance."
So do your smiles give you balance, My dear.
"Don't let me fall into the trap of taking myself too seriously. Help me keep the proper perspective about all You have told me in these past few days. Please help me keep my sense of proportion and balance."
That comes from keeping a sense of humor, My dear. Do you recall the marching cats?
"Yes, that was funny."
So if you find yourself thinking too seriously, find something to laugh about. OK?
"OK. How about right now?"
That would be a good idea.
"Thank You."
My dear?
"Yes?"
Laugh with Me too. Let Me in on the fun, OK?
"Always."
Thanks, My dear. Come.
"Yes, Lord. It is sometimes funny to me how matter-of-fact You are, or lighthearted about some things that would seem to require more seriousness. I guess that is part of my folly."
Seriousness sometimes gets in the way of My revelation, dear. You will understand this more in time too. There is not enough laughter among those who believe themselves to be dedicated to the truth. There needs to be lightheartedness in truth seeking, dear. Do you believe this?
"Yes, Lord. You are joy as well!"
Yes, dear. So what do you think I like to see in My followers?
"A sense of humor and an attitude that allows mistakes and laughter at mistakes. Also, as you have shown me, you like to see the kind of acceptance that allows others to be less than perfect. I think You like to see cheerfulness in Your followers, and honesty about life and feelings.

I suspect it pleases You greatly whenever one of Your followers willingly shares in another person's burden, thus lightening it, without need of recognition or reward. The sharing is simply out of love and a desire to ease the pain of a fellow being."

Go on, dear. You are telling the truth.

"I want to hear You tell me what You like to see—if You want to tell me, that is. Otherwise I will continue."

Where do you think you are getting these thoughts?

"From You?"

Yes. So continue, knowing I am guiding your pen.

"Yes, Lord. I think it pleases You when there is no judgment or criticism of others in the hearts of Your followers—when actually those thoughts just do not enter. And if another judgmental person plants such thoughts, they are turned around and even sent away. I think You like to see happiness in Your followers and lots of smiling, real smiling that comes from a heart in love with You. That kind of smiling makes changes happen, I think, because it carries Your blessing. I have always thought You like to see Your followers smooth the way for others who are having difficulty, whatever it may be, again without any need for recognition or reward. I think You like to see Your followers live Your words more than speak them. Your followers who repeat Your words but do not heed any call to live Your meaning miss Your point. I think You wish they would get it. I feel as if I have written enough on this for now. Have I?"

Yes, dear.

Chapter Twenty

Jesus,
How blessed I am
To love You
Though my love is so little.
But You like littleness,
I know.

You said,
Bring the little ones
To Me.

Oh my Jesus, let me
be little.

Let me live and love
As freely, as joyfully,
Yet as seriously as a child.

Let me bring You joy
As a child!

Good morning, My precious dear. Today shall be a blessed day. Let go now, My dear. Go about your day unconcerned with anything except My loving you. Let all things flow from this.

"Yes, with pleasure!"

My loving you gives you pleasure, but does it not also keep you in pleasure?

"Yes, Lord."

Do you see how My love is never ending? Do you see how My love is continuous and all fulfilling because it lasts and keeps increasing and becoming ever new?

"Yes, Lord. But today I shall let go and let You convince me of all this."

So be it. Now, breathe My name for a little while, and anchor your heart in My love. We are one in this, My dear.

"How precious is this gift You give."

How precious is this gift you give Me.

"What gift?"

Your letting go and letting Me. This allows Me the pleasure of showing you My way in all events, in all things, in all relationships. My way, My dear, is love.

"I know, Lord. I know. Teach me more."

Come. Let us enjoy your morning coffee together. My dear?

"Yes, Lord?"

I feel such delight when you share little things with Me—little pleasures, little joys, little ways. I repeat, I like little. I feel a part of you in littleness. Do you understand?

"Tell me more."

I am infinity itself, so I am not impressed by greatness. What impresses Me and gives Me delight is love in littleness. The more intricate, the sweeter—intricate where you enter into awareness of the simplest, smallest matter as being of Me and in Me. For instance, suddenly you are aware of Me in washing one fork or in folding one piece of clothing, or in touching a stranger's arm, or in an exchange of smiles, or in conversation with one who is troubled. You feel Me, you love Me, and you call My name in all these many little ways. Keep on, My dear! Love me in little ways.

"Again I say, with pleasure!"

Again I say, in pleasure. Come.

"You are so sweet, so very, very gentle and sweet, so tender, so intimate."
You enjoy Me thus?
"Oh Lord, You know I do."
Then tell Me! You long for your dearest to tell you what you long to hear and know. So do I long for you to tell Me what I long to hear. Though I know it, I await your telling Me with sweetest anticipation.
"You do? I'm amazed by You sometimes. How very much in need You are though You have everything at Your fingertips."
I have everything except that which I want the most: the little love of My people, My children, My lovers. That I must await.
"Oh my God, how I long to fill Your need! How I long to give my little love to You, oh lonely one. Let me love You."
With pleasure!
"In pleasure?"
Yes, My sweet, in pleasure. Come. In this pleasure we shall enjoy each other's love.
"I come."
First, breathe My name.
"Yes, Lord. I love You."
I love you, Marie dear.

☙❧

My adored,
I thank You
For all Your gifts,
Precious and pure.

The simple
And the profound.

For the miracle
That I might

Live
In Your presence
In spite of
My littleness.
But I hear You saying,
I love your littleness.
Teach me Your ways,
Oh Lord my God.

I yearn to know
And love You
With all my heart and soul.

Teach me how I might
Receive You
And love You in this
Joyous reception.

Be ever and ever mine!

"Thank You, my Lord, for all You tell me, for all You give me, for all You do for me. Thank You!"

You are welcome. It is My pleasure. Why do you find this humorous, My little one? You should follow My example and always be courteous, most especially with those who are dearest to you.

"Sometimes I am so amazed by the way You talk to me."

You used to have a preconceived idea of Me. Now you are learning more about Me, getting to know Me. Stay open. Do not put Me into a form. Be open, and you shall know Me as I am.

"Oh Lord, already I adore You. I love You as I know You now, but I long to know You more deeply and more intimately, oh my beloved Lord God!"

I long for the same, child, only...

"Only what?"

Only I must wait for you.

"I don't want to make You wait. What is in the way?"
You are not ready. There is much to work on, but fear not. Soon is not far off!
"Thank You. My Lord?"
Yes?
"Show me how to be ready."
Come to Me. Come here first, child, and then do your writing. Make each day a new day. Let My love be for you ever new.
"What now, my Jesus?"
Keep working on balance, My dear, and keeping our communication open and ongoing. If anything causes you doubt, distress, or confusion, give it to Me. Hand everything over to Me. Let Me take care of all your needs. Surrender your all to Me, and I shall make your all become Me. Do you see how this process is changing your life?

"Jesus, I see how the moments are becoming filled with You, thus so are all my hours, days, weeks, months, and years. Now all I seek to change is that my seconds be filled with You as well. Truly You have blessed me, and how I wish just to let go and let You take over completely."

I am, My dear. Let Me now fill your seconds until every instant you are one with Me. All becomes all. I become all in oneness…you and I…one…one…always, always, always one.
"My Lord and my God."
My precious, precious child.

☙❧

Sweet, sweet love!

Oh, how my heart is
Tenderized
In this love.

A steady, burning flame
Warms me
From within.

Marie M. Constance

My whole being
Cries out,
"I love You,
My God.
I adore You
In this kingdom
Within!"

Lock the gate
And throw away
The key.
Imprison me
So I'll never, ever
Leave You
In Your kingdom
Within.

Yet You give me
The free will
To enter
Or to leave.

You force nothing
Upon me,
Do You, my Lord?

With all I am,
I pray for Your blessing
That I never lose
My love and longing
For You,
My dearest,
Only You.

Living Reality

You need not look any further than your heart and soul for this truth I wish to reveal to you.

"Isn't that where I have been looking?"

Yes, but your eyes wander. Your thoughts wander to other means, do they not?

"Yes. Help me train my thoughts and my eyes so they become single and one pointed."

I will show you the way, but this is where you must exercise your own will, where you must take the steps. Come. Let us be on our way.

"Bless me now, Lord, with Your touch. So shall I be more determined to exercise my will."

☙❧

Oh, how blessed I am to love
And be loved!
I am in love with
My God
And all He has created
In such blessed,
Blessed beauty,
And my God loves me.

If only others could know
This fullness of being,
This wondrous consolation
In time of confusion and war.

I suppose if I were directly confronted
By the real pain of battle
Or separation,
It would be so very hard
To feel the love of my God,

But I cannot doubt
He would still
Make Himself known to me.

I pray with all my heart,
My dear,
Beloved God,
That You make Yourself known
To all who are now confronted
By the pain of war.

Each and all, my Lord,
My beloved,
Each and every one
And all!

"The whole world is suffering, Lord!"

The whole world is also rejoicing, My dear. It depends on how you look at it.

"Oh Jesus, my most adorable one, give me eyes to see as You want me to see."

This I shall give you, My dear. This I shall give you. Just come into My heart of love. Come. In My heart I shall bestow all My blessings upon you. Come, My dear, come.

"How I long to do just that, but often I start but do not finish."

Come. I shall pick you up and carry you from start to finish because of your love and your desire to please Me, My dear. Just say My name, and let go. I will do the rest.

"Oh my Lord, forever I am Yours."

Yes, and I, My dear, am also yours. Now, come!

CR ⁊O

Living Reality

Oh, such blessed beauty
You so generously
Display for us
Each day,
My God,
My loving God.

How blessed I am
To perceive only You
Everywhere,
All the time.

All beauty is You,
My God,
And how I feel Your touch
In all that surrounds me!

I feel Your hand
As the sunlight warms my cheek.
I feel Your breath
As the sweet air enters my being.
I feel Your embrace
In all that is around me.

Oh, my beloved!
How tender Your caress.

Oh, my beloved,
How blessed I am
To behold You
Within,
Without,
Everywhere.

I love You, my God.
I adore You.
I thank You.

Forever and ever and ever,
Oh, let me sing
Your praise!

"How sweet the songs of the birds, and to think You told me they have joined in this very song of love in my heart for You."

They also join in My song of love for you! All creation sings My song of love in harmony, My child. Tune thy ears to hear. Join in and become one with it.

"Oh Jesus, lead me!"

Come.

"Oh my Lord, I want to please You. I don't want to neglect my duties, but Your sweetness is so desirable here, now, as I sit quietly with You."

Yes, My child, but do I not give you My sweetness no matter where you are or what you are doing? Am I not ever available? Realize we are one— I in you, you in Me always. Yes, I want you to give yourself to Me here, now, in the quiet, in the stillness. And I will prompt you to rise up and be on your way. Yet I will not stay here. I will go with you wherever you go. I want you to think back. Can you recall any time in the past few months, since you have come to Me, that you called and I did not answer?

"No, Lord, never."

So be convinced. We are one! You are pleasing Me. Live moment to moment in Me. You will know what I want of you.

"Thank You. You are so wonderful to me. Thank You!"

Now, you have some time to proceed with your efforts. Use this time wisely. I will guide you. Come.

"I love You. Help me do what You want me to do."

My child, it's not what I want you to do but what I want you to be.

"What do You want me to be, Lord?"

Mine, all Mine.

"I want to be Yours. Reveal Yourself to me, so I may give myself to You."
Keep coming to Me, child, and we shall both have what we want. Love Me, and I shall give My love to you. In this way shall you know Me and give yourself to Me.
"I want to love You more and more."
Come into My heart of love, and we shall love each other. Come!
"My Lord, I love You. Stay with me."
Just talk to Me. Tell Me you love Me. If that's all you can think to say, then say it over and over again. I never tire of hearing it.

CR ℘

My sweet Lord,
How wonderfully You fill my heart
With such tenderness.

As soon as I look inward,
I find You waiting.
I know it is You
By the intoxicating stir within.

How can this be
So wonderfully true?

Stay with me, dearest.

"Lord, may we continue the conversation we had yesterday about the magnetic pull?"
Yes. I am glad you want to talk about this.
"Tell me more, please."
You see, My dear child, I long for all to be drawn to the center where I am. Distractions draw them away from the center, but love draws them to it. Love, My child, is the shortcut.
"You cannot resist love, can You?"

Marie M. Constance

Love cannot resist itself, child.
"Then I will take the shortcut!"
You already do, My dear one. You do!
"Thank You, my dear Lord, for showing me the way."
Thank you for listening. Thank you for loving.
"You don't look at the times when I was not loving, do You?"
I look at your loving. It makes up for all the rest.
"I haven't really done much."
But you have given Me your heart, and that is what I want most.
"In giving you my heart, I have become the happiest person."
I also want your happiness, My dear little one, My Marie. You see, it pleases Me most when My little ones give themselves to Me. Only then am I able to bestow My happiness on them.

"All this talk about suffering and sorrow as companions along the way—I do not want that. Nobody wants to suffer, but if necessary, I guess I would be willing."

Right now, My child, I want you to feel the highest joy in knowing My love and Me. Live each day, each moment in Me, in My love, in My joy.

"Endless thanks, my beloved Lord, my wondrous God. My lover divine!"

಄ৎ

> The bare trees
> Silhouetted against
> These painted skies
> Hold in their branches—
> A message of hope,
> Of the new life to come.
>
> They hold beauty as well
> In their graceful lines.

Living Reality

Your life force does flow,
Continuing
Even in winter.

These trees reveal more to my heart
Now in their naked truth
Than later
In their clothed fullness,
In greenery.

I feel akin to the trees.

My veins,
Like these branches,
Hold Your life, my God.
All living things hold Your life!

"My Lord, I hesitate to pray for rain—and lots of it—when so many people elsewhere are suffering from too much. Do You wish to instruct me on this? I know You tell me not to be troubled by the world's imbalances, but I wish You to show me the right attitude and the right prayer."

I've been waiting for you to ask this, My dear. The suffering of humanity has always been the hardest thing to accept about this world, hasn't it?

"Yes, Lord."

Trust that I know everything there is to know about any and all suffering, My dear, and trust that I shall give you better understanding as you grow to be more complete in your awareness of Me in all things. I cannot give all understanding to you now, yet you understand more now than you used to. Is this not true?

"It is, Lord."

Do you have more peace about the world's suffering?

"Yes, Lord."

Strive to keep your heart in peace and happiness always, even when you see and hear of suffering. Yet do not cease to pray for an end to all suffering, My dear. Always pray for all to live in peace. Strive for more-complete awareness of Me everywhere, at all times, by staying in this that you know as My peace and My love. This shall help your fellow man far more than dwelling on sadness and suffering. Dwell in Me for them all!

"Yes, Lord."

In time you shall better understand. As for rain, pray for it where it is needed. Also pray for those who are troubled by too much rain. Balance your life and offer it to Me. Let it be part of the microcosm. The world needs balance too. All imbalance is but manifestations of the imbalances in people's lives. Do your part, My dear, and I shall multiply this as well.

"Yes, Lord."

Now, My dear, it is time to put away your pen and seek to balance your day's activities. Let go, and let Me be your guide.

"Yes, Lord."

Come.

෧ɞ

>Oh, my Lord,
>Never let my tears
>Hide Your face from me.
>
>Let them wash away
>All impurities
>From my sight.
>
>Let my tears
>Be Your tears,
>Oh Lord,
>And cleanse me
>In Your love.

Living Reality

As I let my tears flow freely,
Spontaneously,
From within my depths,
I thought that tears of anguish
May very well
Place a veil over my eyes,
Hiding my Lord from me.

Yet pure tears of love for my Lord,
Of joy in perceiving His love for me—
These pure tears cleanse
And purify my heart,
Drawing me closer
And closer
To Him.

Oh, how I adore You,
My Lord and my God!

Already I have used your tears, child. Now, come and let Me use your joy.

"Use me in whatever way You wish. I want to write down what You revealed to me, but already it is gone from my mind."

Your mind does not always comprehend what I reveal to you. That is why I always say, "Come," so you will comprehend with your innermost being. Do not be distressed if you do not remember with your mind what your soul knows.

"I am only distressed when I do not follow Your instructions completely."

I repeat, be patient. Each effort will enable you to follow more completely. Each step. Watch with joy, as I do, the beauty of the unfolding.

Lesson Eight: Stay

Stay in My joy. Stay in My love.
Stay in My embrace.

Chapter Twenty-one

Pondering the meanings of these lessons, I realize lesson eight, "Stay," is really a combination of all the other lessons together. Every day is a rededication to staying in and with Him. As I try to remain mindful that each day may be a new beginning on the spiritual path, I find countless opportunities to live a daily renewal of my commitment to stay in His joy and His loving embrace.

Through repeated efforts to follow the lessons, even if I'm not always successful, I grow more aware of the loving presence of God. I do so in lesson one by keeping my mind on Him and directing all my thinking to Him. In lesson two I do so by humbly accepting what may come each day while trusting He is attentive to all things. In lesson three I remain steadfast on the path while striving to remain in His presence, aware of Him in all beings, all things, and all events. In Lesson Four I receive in Him while keeping an open heart so His love and grace may flow through to those in my heart and prayer, and those I encounter each day.

In lesson five I become aware by realizing how His love is manifested through acts of love. Lesson six speaks to remaining in His actively loving me and my actively receiving Him both within and without. In lesson seven I strive for a balanced attitude toward life through integration of meditation, prayer, and work. And finally, in lesson eight, I become more aware of God's loving presence by practicing each of these lessons while walking hand in hand with Him, thus staying in His loving presence always, always, always.

What an eternal sunrise is this life I live, daily, hourly, moment to moment, in my beloved forever. How happy I am in my God! I feel so privileged, so extremely blessed, and so incredibly gifted by God to be in this process of writing about Him. I am melting in His smiling presence and am filled with awe and gratitude. I feel His laughter now and sense that endearing twinkle in His eyes. I feel that precious, precious presence of one so incredibly intimate and dear. I feel that one smiling through divine tears too, tears that tell of the most wonderful, all-fulfilling love that all shall someday know. But I also feel tears of longing that say, *I wish they only knew what you know, My dear.* Then the sweetest, sweetest person in all of forever reaches out and places His gentle hand upon my tingling head and blesses me. Oh, I feel this. I feel the blessing. Oh, what an incredible wonder!

How my Lord continues to take me into the most blessed state of being. Right now I am so drunk with love. My entire being is simply melting into liquid love. In this state I am totally in His hands. It is the most tender, most pleasurable, most blessed, and most wondrous place. Am I dreaming? No matter what is going on around me, I am in an almost constant state of blissful immersion in pure love divine. At times I'm in such a state of contentedness that all I can do is be, completely accepting any and all things. I am so immersed in all the good that it seems no opposite can enter!

I feel as if I could just fling aside all reserve and hesitation to let go and accept without question all He has told me of myself and of Him! Then, as my heart's arm swings back, what do I find gathered in the swing? The same that I flung aside! This swinging must end soon. When He proclaimed to me, *You are just about to fly*, I replied, "Well, that's different from swinging, isn't it?" Swinging suggests a force that goes back and forth or causes such motion. But flying is free! It is not controlled by such a force at all. In flight, if one's wings are strong and light, one does not have to give in to the forces of gravity and inertia, but one is free as a bird to fly where the wind wills. Oh, to be caught by the wind of God's will, never, ever to be dragged back by my own inertia and gravitational pull to the familiar, the known, the sure. Oh, to let go of the swing once and for all! To let go and surrender myself to the lift and will of the wind, my own God, who is love. Is this, I wonder, what He is proclaiming when He says, *You are just about to fly*?

Once, while walking among the trees, I spotted a feather on the ground. As I picked it up, admiring not only its beauty but also its exquisite design, He began to instruct me. When I heard Him say, *Be as light as this feather, My dear*, I knew He wanted me to let go of worries and fears and lighten up. He helped me see I had been feeling heaviness from worries I needed to give to Him and told me not to forget He is always with me, ever ready to ease any burdens I may be carrying on this path.

He tells me, *You shall embark on an incredible journey.* What am I to make of that? If this voice, which I believe is that of my very own Lord, is telling me this, why should I not dance and shout for joy and proclaim in turn, again, "Yes, Lord. Yes! Yes! Yes!"

Yet I have not yet truly let go. I have not yet stopped swinging. I have not yet received wings that are strong and light enough for me to take flight. But I do believe I shall! I shall fly, and I shall embark on an incredible journey, but in the swinging I ask those gravitational questions, seeking familiar ground and dimension. I ask: "When?" and "Where?" and "How?" I think I have let go of "Why?" That is the first step, perhaps, and now maybe the other questions, though unanswered, will fade away too. I hope so! I want to stop swinging. I want to let go. I want to fly. I want to go on this journey. I pray that I may let go of those questions, let go of the desire for familiars, let go of the need for understanding and certainty, and, in the true spirit of adventure in flight, welcome the unknown, the unfamiliar, and uncertainty, thus welcoming the journey because I know one solid truth that is certain and familiar: He loves me and holds me always.

I know God's love. I know His voice. I know His embrace. In this knowing I believe His words are true as well. If I believe I hear His voice then I believe the words He speaks. I must! I have no choice, really, but to believe and receive the wings He holds out to me now. Be gone, all fear. Be gone, all doubt. Be gone, all hesitation. Come, all truth. Come, all peace. Come, all wisdom, to me. Show me the way I am to go.

Just take My hand, I hear Him say. *Take My hand. Receive My kiss. Be transformed by My touch. Come. Receive My grace, My gift of flight. Receive these wings of light!*

How incredible is this life I lead, this unbelievable existence in God. God! Oh, wonder of wonders. Oh, joy of joys. Sweetest tears flow unceasingly now from that blessed wellspring within, of awe, of wonder, of gratitude, and of love. Divine love is imprisoning me, and there is no escaping His tremendous hold on my heart and soul. I'm forever and ever in love with my God, and the wonder of it all is that for every breath of love I offer, I receive hurricanes that swirl and whirl, and tornadoes lift up all in my heart and carry it into a heavenly kingdom where all is beauty, all is joy, and all is light, truth, peace, wisdom, and love divine forever. Such is the nature of the love He is revealing to me. Such is the love that is in me! Such is the love I feel. I exist in this world with all mankind, yet here, within, all exists in Him, in light, in peace, in love. Oh, He is all, and beyond all is He!

My whole being is permeated by the sweetest happiness full of hope realized. Am I the happiest person on Earth? My God is filling me to overflowing with such incredible hope of what is to be for all. For all! Oh, the happiness all shall know. Tears of such incredible peace, such complete gratitude, and such tremendous hope as well as tears of sweetest, sweetest love for a God so generous and kind stream down my cheeks. Oh, to feel and know what is to be. Almighty God! All the pain and suffering that has ever been cannot compare to the overwhelming light and love, happiness and peace there will be for all.

What a wonderful reality! Sometimes, when situations in this world seem very bleak, I remind myself of the hope found in the truth underlying all: God is. Though darkness, destruction, and desolation are found in this world, ultimately God is in this world and contains this world. He is above and around and under and beyond and through all. God, the ultimate good, is forever and ever, and always was and always will be. That is the good news!

There is, in fact, so much goodness in the person of this God I have come to know that I could never contain it within the substance of letters and books composed of words, except by His grace. Because of the very goodness of my God, He comes through to anyone desiring to receive Him. I shall continue in this effort to write about Him, trusting always that all who read His words may receive Him in the essence.

Chapter Twenty-two

So much love fills my heart.

The only release I have
At this moment
Is my tears.

Let me water these precious flowers
I place at Your feet
With my tears.

Oh, transform them, my Lord,
Tears of my eyes,
Salt and water,
To tears of my soul,
Living water
And sweetest joy.

"Oh my Lord, 'Stay'?"
    Yes, My dear. Yes! You have heard, and you shall know the meaning of this word that defines lesson eight: stay.

Living Reality

"My Lord and my God."

My dear, dear child.

"My Lord God, will You stay too?"

I never leave.

"If I have a part to play, please let me know what it is."

Your part, My dear, is to stay in Me always.

"Yes, Lord. I love You. I love and adore You! Stay as close as You are now."

I am always this close, My child. Never forget this. Though there will be times when you do not feel this close to Me, realize that in truth you are always in Me, and I am always in you with just as much love. I will always love and cherish you, My dear little one.

"If only I could give myself to You fully now."

You may give yourself to Me now in surrendering to whatever comes your way, in staying in Me no matter what, no matter where. Stay in Me.

"I'll try with all I am."

That's all I ask! Do not permit yourself to fall into doubt and discouragement though all outer forces may try to bring you down. Remain steadfast in Me, in My peace. If you feel you are slipping away, turn and run to Me quickly. You will find Me ever ready to shelter you. Mark My words: stay in Me!

"Hold my dear ones, Lord. Hold them tenderly."

This you must do too, My dear child. You must hold them in your heart even in the midst of pain and confusion. You must constantly pray and love, listen and love.

"Tell me something I may write to turn to time and time again, especially if I am tempted to doubt the reality of You and Your presence."

Oh, My dear, sweet child, feel My tenderness, feel My sweetness, feel My love for you. Your heart is feeling My presence now, is it not? And sweet tears fill your eyes. You know I love you. You know it! Never, ever doubt I am always here, in you, with you, for you. Believe in Me though others do not. And ask for the grace to love, the grace to let My love flow through your heart to theirs. Oh, My child, how I love you! How very completely do I love you.

"Bless them now, Lord. Bless them now."
I will, dear one. I will.

☙❧

My dear one,
How long have I strayed?

Keep me now
Ever close to You,
Ne'er to part
From Your ever-loving heart.

"Lord, You know everything about me, even that which I do not know myself."
Yes, My dear. I love you. Do you know all about this?
"What I know already is incredibly wondrous. Thank You."
My dear, the things I ask of you are on many levels. Sometimes more emphasis is on one level than another, or something is expressed more on one level than another. Simply because I have asked these things of you does not mean you are able to respond on all levels at once, with equal intensity, all the time. I do not expect this of you.
"Then tell me, please, what You expect."
Ah, My dear, I was waiting for this question.
"Will you tell me now?"
Yes, but as I tell you with words, please, My dear, hear My meaning as well.
"Yes, Lord, I shall listen with my heart while You speak."
Always, My dear, always listen with your heart. Now, for your answer, My dear. Do you know what I really expect of you?
"No, but I hear Your answer already. I hear the meaning."
Yes, My dear. I expect nothing from you or of you, but I offer everything. The fulfillment of all your dreams, all your longings, My dear Marie, all your desires I offer to you. Does that ease your concern at all?

"You know it does, my Lord. You know it does. Thank You for being so very, very sweet and so incredibly generous!"

It is My delight to please you, Marie, My pleasure to ease your doubts, fears, and worries, My joy to bring you happiness, My goal to give you My love. Come. Please Me, delight Me, bring Me joy, and help Me reach My goal. Let Me love you.

"Oh Jesus, how can it be so good? It is because You are good. You are goodness itself, and kindness and tenderness and comfort and joy. You are all that is holy and true. You are You! Oh my Lord, forgive my little ways."

I love little, remember?

"Yes, I remember."

Now, delight Me, Marie.

"I am all Yours. Take me now."

Come. I have something to add, My dear.

"Yes, Lord?"

Though I expect nothing, and I offer everything, still I ask something of you: that you stay, that you let Me love you, and that you bring all in. These things I ask of you, My dear.

☙ ❧

Sometimes I think I'm crazy,
And all this is just a game I play.

Yet when doubts try to creep in,
You always reassure me so sweetly,
My dear, dear one.

Oh, how I love You.
How I adore You.
How I long for You
With all my heart,
Jesus, oh my Jesus,
My Lord.

Marie M. Constance

I want to give Your blessings
To my dear ones,
To share You with them
And make them happy
In You.

Can this be?
Or am I a fool
To believe in such things?

Can I really be Your channel
In spite of myself,
In spite of
All my inconsistencies?

Oh Jesus,
My Jesus,
Use me,
Mold me,
Shape me.

You have melted me
In the fires of Your love.
Now remake me,
Renew me,
And reveal
What You want of me.

Without You I am nothing.
Nothing.
With You I am alive and afire!

Use me as You will,
But let me love You

More and more,
Forever and ever.
Amen!

"Bless those who are in sadness. Bless them with Yourself."
I am blessing them. I am holding them. Do not let the sadness cloud your joy. I want you to be in joy.
"You know I feel Your joy even in the midst of sadness. I still feel Your sweet, sweet love."
Stay in My joy. Stay in My love. Stay in My embrace.
"Thank You, my dear Lord, my sweet one. Thank You."
It is My pleasure.

◌৪০

Everything sings Your name,
My Lord.

How can I stop
Thinking of You?

I've tried to resist You
And Your pull,
Yet You always pull
Harder than I resist.

I'd love
Just
To let go.

Then there would be
No resisting,
No pulling,
Just

One
You and me,
One
Forever and ever.

"Good morning, my dear Lord, my beloved God. I awoke many times last night, and my first awareness was always You. Even that cricket kept repeating Your name!"

It pleases Me when you hear My name as well as call it. Please Me more, My dear.

"Am I pleasing You? Sometimes I let little things enter my mind and then my heart, which causes disturbance in this inner communion we share."

Yes, but you always give your struggles to Me, dear.

"Do I really, Lord? I know I tell You, 'Here, take this,' but I don't feel as if I truly give to You all that gets in the way."

It is a process too, My dear. You are learning more and more how to do this. I repeat: Do not expect to master this all at once.

"OK. Thank You."

There. I like to feel your smile, My dear. Though it is only appearing slightly on your face, how it lights up in your heart! I like this.

"It is You, Lord. You are the cause of all my smiles."

I know. Continue to let Me cause your smiles, My dear. I shall cause you great joy.

"I know. You already have!"

Prepare to know more joy, My dear.

"How?"

Remain in My loving you, in My peace, in My joy, and in My will as you know more what it is, for all is perfectly balanced in Me. Thus you shall most gracefully fall into balance as you stay in Me. It is all very simple, all so very easy in Me.

"I know, Lord. Make it easy for all."

I desire this, My dear. More shall know because of your surrender to My will in you. Play the part I have given you well, and all shall benefit from it. If only all would play their parts well too and see that I give them their parts. They need to know this, My dear. Never fear remaining firm in this conviction.

"Thank You always for Your counsel and Your wisdom revealed in Your guiding hand, but most of all thank You for Your love."

And most of all, thank you for your love, My dear little one, My Marie dear.

☙❧

My Lord,
I would love You
With all my heart and soul
If I were more awake in You.

Yet as much as I may be able
To offer now,
I give
Totally,
Without reserve.

*Sweet, sweet, sweet
Is thy caress.*

These words come to me now.
Oh Lord, reveal their meaning!

Live each day to the fullest, My dear. Live in eager desire to do whatever you need to do to follow Me. Live in keen awareness of My hand in all things, all events, all that is before you. See My hand thus, and see Me in all My children. Try to see Me in all you meet. Think of Me, talk to Me, especially when you meet new people. Always ask for My blessing on them. This is yet another way to take My hand. Be aware of Me everywhere, at all times.

"Jesus, my dear loving one, sometimes when I'm talking to You, I'm not attentive to those around me. I so desire to hold a conversation with You, I tune out all others. Please, guide me so I will be more attentive to those around me and realize I am actually being attentive to You then, and so I may wait until alone to be so absorbed in You. Please guide me, Lord."

I am guiding you. I want you to be absorbed in Me. So many are absorbed in other things and forget I am there. But you, My dear, never forget Me, and you are ever seeking to hear My voice. This pleases Me, as does your loving. I do not mind that you love certain ones so intensely. From where do you think this love comes?

"You!"

Yes, and you are doing My will when you love those who are so dear to you with your heart, and even though you are apart, you continue to love them. This pleases Me too. Do not worry about being attentive. You are doing fine. You are attentive enough. Just keep on being so attentive to Me. Great shall be your reward, My dear.

଴ଃ ଓ

    Up and down,
    Wave after wave,
    Will this ever
    Cease?
    Will I ever
    Even out,
    Become calm?

    I guess it's up to me.

    You are ever here.
    I must respond.

My dear?
"Yes, my Lord?"

Do you enjoy My company?

"You know I do!"

Then why don't you seek to make this enjoyment more constant? Increase your enjoyment of My continual presence, and I shall increase your joy. You may increase your enjoyment by increasing your awareness of Me, and you may do this by coming in more often, more deeply, more intensely, and for longer periods of time. Yet always remember intensity can and will be of utmost importance. Time is less important. My dear, letting go is also a means to My grace, to increasing your enjoyment of My constant presence. Do you understand?

"I think so. Do I?"

Yes. You are also increasing in understanding. Rejoice, I say. Rejoice! I am forever loving you, and I am always here awaiting you. Give Me joy too, My dear, in your constancy.

"I want more than anything to please You, Lord, to give to You. If I may give You joy, then I'll be more constant."

You are constant already in your unwavering devotion to Me. The lack of constancy has come from your unwillingness to let go, but this too we shall overcome together. You will want to let go simply because you know it is the best way. So just cooperate with Me in this, and all shall increase in goodness. Now, My dear, come, rest in Me. Enjoy being with and in Me. Receive!

"Receive me too, Lord."

I am receiving you. Come.

ॐ

>The intensity is returning,
>Yet so sweet is the divine giver,
>It is never too much to bear,
>And if it approaches extremes,
>He so graciously calm the seas
>With sweet, sweet peace for a time,
>Until the tempestuous intensity
>Of love returns.

Oh, He is.
He lives.
He loves.
He loves me!

I swim.
I melt.
I fly.
I become.

Oh, to know
His blessed will,
To be in
His blessed embrace,
To be in
His blessed will,
To know
His blessed embrace.

Oh, to be.
Oh, to know.
Oh, to love!

Remember when I told you I shall reveal Myself to you, but then I told you that you are not yet ready for great light?

"Yes, I remember."

And since then I have told you that you are ready. Just receive! Now, I tell you again: you are ready. Receive My light, My dear, for I am light.

"Oh my Lord, I am at Your feet. Show me Your light if that is Your desire. Show me if I am ready to see, ready to receive. Just hold me, for even though You say I am ready, it is hard for me to comprehend what that means. I don't feel any more ready, but if You say I am, I must believe You. Just show me the right attitude too, the one that is best in this readiness. Is it an attitude of waiting, of anticipation, of receptivity, or of surrender? Tell me please, Lord."

You have described the best, My dear, in all of the above. However, you left out the most important aspect of the best attitude. Can you guess what that might be?

"Yes, Lord. I know. It is love! The attitude of divine love and all that encompasses it. I see that all of the above are simply parts of the whole. That is all I need to know, all I need to do, all I need to be: love!"

Yes, My dear, for I am love. Know Me. Act Me. Live Me. Be Me. In other words, know love. Act love. Live love. Be love! Be a living embodiment of love, My dear. Remember this.

"Yes, my Lord, yes! Just keep me ever in Your embrace, and I shall be all You want me to be."

ଔଃ

My heart is so full of love,
The richest, most wonderful love!
I can hardly contain it,
But I yearn for more.

I perform my tasks as best I can,
But it is difficult to move.

I just want to be still
And drink in this
Wondrous nectar
Of my God
And give Him
My full attention.

Yet I know
He wants me to work
Around the home.

Marie M. Constance

You are working for Me
In all you do no matter
How small the task.

What bliss
At Your touch of love
So dear!

Endless thanks to You,
Oh, my dearest,
My most blessed lover.

Forever be my love divine!

Let me be with You
Just a little longer, my Lord,
Just a little longer,
Then I'll get back to work.

Let me love You
Now, my Lord,
Right here
And now.

I am pleased you have let go and let Me. Now, My dear, I know you have many things you feel you should do today, but you also feel pulled to My loving you within, in stillness. Which do you think I would prefer you do?

"Oh Lord, I know what You want now that You have brought it into this conversation. I know You want me to let go and let You love me."

Yes, My dear. The rest shall be waiting for you as always, but when I desire your company in stillness, and I give you the time, then rejoice and receive My gifts of time, quiet, and most of all My love.

"Oh my Jesus, then take me, for I am Yours, letting go, letting You."

Let go of your pen too, My dear.
"With pleasure."
Come! Without delay now. Come.
"Yes, Lord, without delay."

Chapter Twenty-three

My God caresses me
In the breezes.
He tickles me in the
Reflected sparkles
Along the water's edge
And in dewdrops upon leaves.

He sends me soaring
In the magnificence
Of mountains receding.

He lifts me high,
So high,
Through clouds
And splendor in colors
Of the setting sun.

I am so blessed
To be touched,

To be lifted,
To be caressed
By Him!

"Oh Jesus, how I feel Your love. How I feel Your touch, Your caress. Oh, how my entire being simply turns to liquid love in Your loving me."

Yes, My dear. Thus you become what I will you to become: a living embodiment of love! You are this, My dear. You cannot deny it, can you?

"No, Lord, I feel this. I feel only this: love divine. And I enter into such a blessed space, such a blissful realm, oh my Lord, my God."

This space, My dear, this realm, is your home. Welcome, My dear. Welcome home!

"Almighty God, take me in. Keep me forever and ever here, in You, at home."

Enjoy the present moment, My precious. Enjoy the present moment.

"Oh my Lord, in enjoying the present moment, I am enjoying You."

Precisely, My dear. Now, enjoy Me more. I am dying to give My life to you.

"Oh my Jesus, make me able to enjoy more. Make me able to receive more. I'm not sure I can contain any more. I am ready to burst!"

Then become this. Remember, you are not containing, you are becoming.

ଔଓ

How my entire being is captivated
Just by thinking of Him.

I am flooded with love!

Such tenderness envelops my heart,
Such sweet, sweet tenderness.

Marie M. Constance

I am not sure
What to do.

I am at a loss for words.

I can only perform if He leads me.
Otherwise I collapse,
For with such overwhelming force
This flood comes
Gushing through.

He must sustain me
And guide me
Every step of the way,
So His love might flow through.

May I thus be integrated,
So the inner
And the outer persons
Become one?

That which you seek in solitude is to be found amid the crowds.
"Lord, sometimes You say, *Come in,* and then someone needs my attention. Please, instruct me."
You must be ever ready to meet the needs that arise in your surroundings, in your home, in your place of work, wherever you are. You may continue to converse with Me no matter what, but you must wait to come into the stillness. Be ever receptive, no matter where you are or what you are doing. Come into My embrace in the stillness of the morning and the night. Remain in My embrace even in the midst of activity. When I say, "Come in," you may do that in activity, in quiet, in stillness. Even in the midst of chaos, My dear, you may come in.
Isn't this already becoming a reality for you? Yet before, you always separated. My dear, integrate your being so you are always in Me. I can show you this, My dear, but it is a process. Do not lose heart! Believe Me. You are

becoming. I see things about you that you do not see. Continue to let go and let Me. Continue to converse with Me. Continue, My dear, to grow in grace and love.
"Yes, Lord."
Now, come in.
"Yes, Lord."
No matter what, stay in. Remain in My loving you.
"Yes, my loving Lord."

◯₃ ॐ

>Oh, dear one,
>Lover of my soul,
>King of my heart.
>
>Forgive me for my failings,
>Especially for failing
>To love You
>With my whole heart,
>Mind, and Soul.
>
>Show me how to love You, Lord.
>Let me please You.
>Let me see Your smile.
>Find Your pleasure in me.
>Oh, lover divine!

My dear, I want you to enter My smile. Find the true meaning of the smile you felt as I prompted you to tell Me your thoughts and as you felt My desire to tell you more. Enter My smile! Know Me in this, for I am forever smiling upon you, My dear.
"Yes, Lord, thank You."
Come in.
"Reveal to me the meaning of Your smile."
Come.

Marie M. Constance

Oh blessed Jesus,
I long to be ever and ever
Absorbed in the thought of You,
Consumed by love for You.

Oh, how my soul takes flight
In the single thought
Of You.
Just You!

My wings are made
Of Your love.
The breezes that lift me,
Your joy.
My horizon, my goal,
My destination
Your embrace.

All that You
Reveal to me,
My beloved,
Is ever so precious,
Ever so sacred,
Ever so new.

You lift me up
And carry me away
On the wings of love.

I fly with You
In the heights
Of joy,

And then, how
Softly we land,
You and I together,
On solid ground
To do Your will.

Stay with me,
My beloved,
And show me Your will.

My dear, do you know that your "yes" is sweet music to My ears? I cherish it and its meaning, and I bless you whenever you say it. I love you, Marie. I love you. Now, do you want to know more of My meaning in this sweet song I sing to you always?

"Oh Jesus, the meaning comes pouring into my heart and soul as I hear and feel Your song of love. Sweet, blissful music!"

Marie, listen and become. Yes, this is what I desire now. This is My wish, My request, My desire—that you listen to My song of love and become the meaning.

"Oh Jesus, I feel it already. Show me how to become, to hold and be at the same time that which I feel within: Your love. Show me, Jesus, how to become love."

Let go, My precious. Just fly, as I have instructed you already, with Me and into Me. Feel My love filling you as it lifts you. Let your wings unfold now, and fly in your unfolding, in My enfolding you in and with wings of love. Oh, My precious, let go, let Me. Oh, enter. Receive. Be. Become this that I am in you. Become love. Become one with Me in love. Become Me, My dear. I long for you. Come.

"My precious, precious God, my life, my love, my all, my very own."

Know how much I love you, dear. Know I am love. Know I am this in you. Enter love. Enter Me. Be one with love, with Me. Become love and know how much I love you. Know Me.

"And my Lord, I shall not only know You, I shall love You!"

Come. Let go. Be. Love.

Marie M. Constance

☙❧

Sweet river
Ever flowing within.

Gift of my Lord.
Drown me,
Take me,
Engulf me.

Let me ever and ever
Taste and drink
From You!

Never would I thirst again
If I could but once
Deeply,
Deeply
Drink from You.

Oh, river of life.
I love You,
Your source,
Your mouth,
Your depths,
Your all!

"The essence of being in You is sweet, sweet love and deep, deep joy."
I want You to drink in this essence, My child. Drink until you are full! And then expand your capacity so you may drink more. Keep coming to Me, and drink your fill.
"My Lord, my life, my love, my joy!"
My dear child, let us talk about how you might keep My love alive in your heart no matter where you are or what you are doing.

Living Reality

"I am listening."

First of all, My child, ask for My love, then let it stir up within you a desire to have Me always with you, helping you, living in you. Let My love be the source, the flow, the continuance of all your energy, all your loving. Let Me be the only source. If you feel you have sustenance from another source, see Me in that too. Always look for Me in everything that comes your way. Look for Me, find Me, and live in Me.

"So my Lord, what You are telling me is to ask for Your love first and then look for You in everything, and see everything as coming from You."

Yes, My child, but do not only repeat My words. Live them! Do not be discouraged if you are not able to do everything I tell you immediately and all the time. I do not expect this of you. But I know you are coming to Me, and, as I said before, each time you call My name, we are that much closer to our goal.

"Our goal?"

Oh, yes, My child, our goal! Don't you know I long for you to realize complete union with Me? I long for this more than you do because you do not even know what it means. But I do, and I know all things. I wait for you. I make Myself known to you in ways that are best for you. Do not compare. Do not analyze. Just live in My love and know I am always with you. I love you. I long for You really to come to Me, and you shall.

"Guide me, please. Sometimes I get confused and feel as if I am trying too hard. I guess that is when I compare and analyze."

That is when you stop asking and try to proceed without Me.

"Do I, Lord? I am sorry."

It is part of this stage you are in, My child. Do not let it distress you. Just see it for what it is and let go so you might move on, following My voice, following Me.

"Take me by the hand and lead me now. My hands are free. Take both my hands."

Come, and enjoy the ride.

"The ride?"

Marie M. Constance

Yes, I will carry you now that you have let go. I may now lift you up and carry you.
"Really?"
Yes, really. Now come.

☙❦

I hear a voice
Quietly
Whispering.
*"Come in.
Follow the waters in.*

Sweet mountain stream,
Flowing downward
Yet calling me
Upward,
To a higher
Mountain peak.

Oh, cool, refreshing waters
Echo in their
Unwieldy course,
The sound of deeper,
Even more-certain
Waters of purpose.

Oh, water of life.
Oh, blessed fountain
Spilling over
My heart's domain.

Oh, curling stream.
Oh, bubbling brook.

Teach me
The secrets
Of your waters,
So in these
Truths
Reflecting
I will know
My caller's will.

Yet in this knowledge
May I return
Thanks for gifts
Yet to come.

Oh, let my life
Be one resounding
Hymn of gratitude
For all I've known
And all that
Is to be known.

Marie?
"Yes, Lord?"
I love you. Never forget this. No matter what you are experiencing or bringing to Me, whether it is pleasure or pain, bliss or confusion, always know that underlying all is My intense love for you.
"Oh my Lord, I love You too!"
I know. Now, do as I have asked you.
"Yes, Lord, with pleasure."
My sweet, sweet little one, My precious, precious dear, feel and know My love now.
"I do. Oh, how I feel and know and enjoy You."
All is well, My dear. All is well. My dear?
"Yes, Lord?"

It is finished. You may now finish this book. Tell them all, dear, that I am love, and I love all. I want all to come to Me as you have, dear.

"Yes, Lord. Always, always, always: Yes! Yes! Yes!"

My precious little one, keep on telling them all about Me. How I want all to know My love. I give you this task, My dear: tell them all about Me and My love. Tell them all that I am."

"Oh, my heart is on fire my Lord, God. Yes! Yes! Yes! Forever and ever do I surrender to Your love, to all You are, and to all You ask of me. Oh my Jesus, my lover, my one and only one, I love You forever.

I know.

A Divine Plea
Let Me care for you. Let Me love you.

Each and every one of My children has a unique relationship with Me. It is sacred. I cherish each as My own. I call each in a unique way. Though My children's worship of Me has common expressions and forms, I receive the individual devotion that lies deep within each heart. I see the personality of each one as sacred and unique. I rejoice and delight in all My children, and I receive all forms of worship. Whatever My children offer Me, I cherish and receive just as parents rejoice in receiving the gifts their children give. Whether they embody the skills of professional artists or the spontaneity of young children, all gifts are received with delight.

Please, My children, accept and rejoice in your differences as I do, as parents accept and rejoice in the differences in their children. Please, My children, love each other tenderly, treat each other respectfully, and reverently see each other as I see you: as sacred entities of My love. As parents desire their children to treat and love each other in this way, so I long for you to do the same. When parents look upon their children with love, they see them as wonderful reflections of their own love and rejoice in caring for them with unconditional love. So do I rejoice in caring for you. Let Me care for you. Let Me love you, and all I ask in return is that you love each other as I love you, without condition, with all tenderness, respect, and reverence. Realize each and every one of you is unique and sacred, and love each other so.

www.ingramcontent.com/pod-product-compliance
Lightning Source LLC
Chambersburg PA
CBHW022058090426
42743CB00008B/641